C

B'w

NORTHBROOK COLLEGE SUSSEX

Library and Learning Resources: Library

Tel: 01903 273305/273450 or email: bwlibrary@nbcol.ac.uk

This book must be returned to the library, or renewed, on or before the date last entered below.

Renewal can be granted only when the book has not been previously requested by another borrower.

- 8 OCT 2004	- 6 JAN 2009	6.3.18
4 JAN 2006	2 4 JUN 2009	16.4.18 8.5.18
	2/6	25.5.18
4 JAN 2006	- 3 NOV 2014	12.6.18 29.6.18
2 2 NOV 2006	1 3 APR 2015	25p fine +
2 2 MAR 2007	26 APR 2017 0 4 JAN 2018	to return
2 3 APR 2008	24 Jan 18	
2 0 MAY 2008	19.2.18	
- 3 NOV 2008	19.3.18	

PLEASE PROTECT BOOKS FROM DAMAGE   R.7001 SY4

Hodder & Stoughton

Orders: please contact Bookpoint Ltd, 130 Milton Park, Abingdon, Oxon OX14 4SB. Telephone: (44) 01235 827720, Fax: (44) 01235 400500. Lines are open from 9.00–6.00, Monday to Saturday, with a 24-hour message answering service.

British Library Cataloguing in Publication Data
A catalogue record for this title is available from The British Library

ISBN 0 340 78012 6

First published 2000
Impression number   10 9 8 7 6 5
Year   2005   2004   2003   2002

Cartoons by Richard Chapman
Typeset by Transet Limited, Coventry, England.
Printed in Great Britain for Hodder & Stoughton Educational, a division of Hodder Headline plc, 338 Euston Road, London NW1 3BH by Cox & Wyman Ltd, Reading, Berkshire.

CONTENTS

Contents

Who was Freud?

Sigmund Freud was an Austrian doctor. He lived from 1856–1939 and he is famous because he founded a new system of **psychology** that he called **psychoanalysis**.

WHY IS FREUD'S WORK SO IMPORTANT?

Freud totally changed our way of looking at ourselves and our relationships with others. Before Freud, psychologists usually just described and observed behaviour. Freud wanted to go deeper, to analyse and explain it. Psychoanalysis is still the basis of various therapies used today in the treatment of **neurosis** and **psychosis**.

Freud's work largely concerns the **unconscious**. He did not invent the idea of unconscious mental processes – in fact the idea had been around for some time. Even the Latin writer, Juvenal (AD 60–130), thought the idea was not new when he wrote 'from the gods comes the saying "know thyself"'. (This saying was written up in the temple at Delphi, where the famous Oracle was.) But Freud was the first really to apply the idea in his clinical practice and formulate theories about it. He lived at just the right time and place to be able to bring together these previous ideas.

Freud's work with the unconscious made people begin to look at themselves more honestly and see what really goes on under the surface. In many cases this enabled people to move on from unhelpful or damaging ways of thinking and behaving. The new way of looking at things and examining people's motives had its disadvantages too. For example, an unselfish person might be seen as secretly indulging in self-punishment,

KEYWORDS

Psychology: the scientific study of the mind and behaviour.

Psychoanalysis: a system of psychology and method of treating mental disorders.

Neurosis: minor nervous or mental disorder.

Psychosis: severe mental disorder.

Unconscious: parts of the mind and personality of which a person is not aware.

while celibacy might be seen as hiding a fear of sex, or even a nasty perversion of some sort.

Freud said that we have many inner motives for our behaviour, and that these are mostly sexual. There are also other motives, such as power or aggression. Nowadays, Freud is often seen as having claimed that absolutely everything in our minds is sexual. In fact, he realized that not everything could be – otherwise neurotic people would not have to struggle to suppress sexual feelings. Freud was a prolific writer and very good at explaining ideas. This meant that he acquired many followers. His theories have also led to controversy, and from his original work many new strands of psychology have developed.

WHAT IS PSYCHOANALYSIS?

Psychoanalysis is a whole system of psychology that Freud gradually developed as he worked with neuroses and other mental problems. It has three main aspects.

* It is a type of therapy aimed at treating mental and nervous disorders – this is the aspect with which most people are familiar. The therapy is based on **dynamic psychology** and works with theories about the unconscious and the ways in which it interacts with the **conscious mind**. The method is based on a **free association** process. This helps the patient to recall **repressed experiences** and so begin to sort out neuroses.

* It attempts to explain how the human personality develops and how it works.

* It provides theories about how individuals function within personal relationships and in society.

KEYWORDS

Dynamic psychology: method that emphasises that there are motives and drives for behaviour.

Conscious mind: The part of the mind that is aware of its actions and emotions.

Free association: process where the client is given a word and then tells the analyst all the ideas that come to mind.

Repressed experiences: experiences that have been actively pushed out of the conscious mind into the unconscious.

FREUD'S EARLY LIFE

Sigmund Freud was born on 6 May 1856 in Freiberg, Moravia, which was then part of the Austro-Hungarian Empire. The town is now Pribor in the Czech Republic. In 1860 his family moved to Vienna, where he then lived for most of his life. When Freud was born his father, Jakob, was forty and already a grandfather. He was twenty years older than Amalie his second wife, who was Freud's mother. Freud was the first of Amalie's eight children and he was her firm favourite. He later said that this gave him a feeling of invincibility and a great will to succeed.

Young 'Sigi' was a swot at school, and his family was very ambitious for him. He soon mastered Greek, Latin, German, Hebrew, French and English, and by the age of eight he was reading Shakespeare. Needless to say he often came top of his class. He had his own room in the crowded home – all the other lesser siblings had to share. He even ate his evening meal apart from the others, and when his sister Anna's piano playing distracted him from his studies, his parents had the instrument removed from the apartment.

Sigi had his own room in the crowded house.

The family were Jewish by descent, but they did not practice the Jewish religion. Being Jewish was difficult because anti-Semitism was rife in Vienna at the time. Most people in Vienna were Roman Catholics. Two of young Sigi's boyhood heroes were the anti-establishment Oliver Cromwell, and Hannibal, the Carthaginian leader who got the better of the Romans.

Jakob Freud was a wool merchant, but he was not very successful financially. He was married three times and produced many children, meaning that he was unable to support Sigmund financially later on. It is important to be aware of Freud's family background and psychological make-up because they influenced his later thinking.

VIENNA AND THE SOCIETY FREUD LIVED IN

Freud had a sort of love-hate relationship with Vienna. He was often critical about Viennese people and yet he was very reluctant to ever leave. Several aspects of Viennese society were important in influencing Freud.

* It was a very **bourgeois** society.

* It was in a state of economic decline. This led to unemployment, poverty and overcrowding.

> **KEYWORD**
>
> Bourgeois: middle-class materialistic and conservative.

* People had a prudish attitude towards sex. This meant that 'nicely brought-up' girls were appalled when they finally found out about what was going to happen to them. At the same time, there was moral decline that led to widespread prostitution. This was the kind of dual standard in thinking that could have led Freud to ideas about the unconscious.

* Men were still thought of as being highly superior to women. Freud himself did not seem to realize that there was anything wrong with this attitude in his self-analysis. (This just shows how difficult psychoanalysis can be!)

* The prevailing culture was strongly anti-Semitic. This made it hard for the young Freud when he was struggling to advance his career.

* New ideas of social reform were creeping in, such as early feminist ideas and Social Democracy (a form of Marxism).

A BRIEF OUTLINE OF FREUD'S CAREER

Freud's early ambition had been to study law, but when he entered the University of Vienna in 1873 it was to study medicine. Here he became interested in zoological research and spent an obsessive amount of time cutting up eels. He was greatly influenced by one of his teachers, Ernst Brücke, who was dedicated to the **mechanistic** approach. This approach was still unpopular early in Freud's life, because it ruled out religious and **vitalist** thinking in biology. Freud remained a convinced **determinist** throughout his life.

During his clinical training, Freud was influenced by one of his tutors, Theodor Meynert, to specialize in **neurology** and **neuropathology**, finally graduating as a Doctor of Medicine in 1881. He would have liked to stay in research, but growing financial pressures, and the fact that he wanted to get married, meant that he would have to practice as a doctor. He spent the next three years gaining medical experience at the Vienna General Hospital.

KEYWORDS

Mechanistic: seeing a person as a machine whose behaviour is determined by physical or chemical causes.

Vitalist: philosophical idea that assumes non-material forces are at work in biology.

Determinist: someone who believes that all events follow a rigid pattern of cause and effect.

Neurology: branch of biology that studies the structure and functions of the nervous system.

Neuropathology: the study of diseases of the nervous system.

Freud spent some time studying the effects of cocaine, even injecting it into himself. He thought that it was a harmless anti-depressant and a useful anaesthetic. In 1885 it was used on his father to perform a successful eye operation. However, people soon became addicted to the drug and Freud learned the importance of caution when doing scientific research.

In 1885, Freud spent a few months in Paris, studying with a famous neurologist called Jean Martin Charcot. Charcot was experimenting with **hypnosis** to help cases of **hysteria**. Freud's experience here was very important because it led him to the idea that the mind could affect physical symptoms. In 1886 he entered private practice as a neuropathologist and began his own work with hysterics. From this work he developed ideas that were to evolve into psychoanalysis. Right from the start he encountered violent opposition from many other members of the medical establishment, because his ideas were unusual.

KEYWORDS

Hypnosis: a state similar to sleep where the patient is still able to respond to the therapist and is open to suggestions.

Hysteria: a nervous disorder with varying symptoms.

Freud's first published book, *On Aphasia* appeared in 1891 (Aphasia is a neurological disorder where the patient is either unable to recognize words, or unable to pronounce them). This was to be the first of many publications throughout his life. It soon became clear to Freud that psychological disturbances were indeed at work in many cases of mental illness. This idea was to be the basis of his life's work and one of the main ways in which his work was to differ from that of his contemporaries.

At first Freud's work concentrated on looking at the causes and treatment of neurosis. Gradually he expanded his theories and became interested in the way the human **psyche** develops. His work falls into four main phases (see table opposite).

Most of Freud's ideas are explained in his book *The Complete Introductory Lectures on Psychoanalysis*. These were originally published in several separate parts and the ideas were gradually added to and revised.

KEYWORDS

Psyche: the mind, soul or spirit.

Id: the unconscious part of the psyche that is concerned with inherited, instinctive impulses.

Ego: the part of the psyche which reacts to external reality and which a person thinks of as the 'self'.

1886–1894	Studies on the causes and treatment of neurosis, working with neurotic patients. At first Freud concentrated on using hypnosis, but later he developed other forms of therapy which gradually evolved into psychoanalysis.
1894–1900	Freud worked very much alone, doing much self analysis and developing ideas about the sexual origins of neurosis. At the end of this period he produced two very important books, *The Interpretation of Dreams* and *Psychopathology of Everyday Life*.
1900–1914	Freud began to formulate new theories about the origins of neurosis, which led to a whole system of ideas about how the psyche develops from birth onwards. The psychology that he developed at this stage is often called **id** psychology.
1914 onwards	World War I made Freud look at people's behaviour in new ways, as he realized that aggression, as well as sexual urges, could be an important factor in behaviour. He began to develop theories about the whole personality and the ways in which people relate to others. This is known as **ego** psychology

FREUD'S PRIVATE LIFE

In 1886 Freud married Martha Bernays. They had six children, the youngest of whom, Anna, became a psychoanalyst. The family went through a great deal of financial struggle and in 1918 Freud lost a lot of money that had been bound up in Austrian state bonds. Martha insisted that in the 53 years of their marriage they never spoke an angry word. This might be seen as a little suspicious! Apart from letters to friends, Freud was a private person he did not reveal many personal details.

In academic circles, Freud was often seen as being opinionated and rather unconventional, and so much of his work was done in what he called 'splendid isolation'. He obviously had outstanding intellect, but, by his own admission, he had a rather neurotic, obsessive personality. He was the kind of person who has to do everything meticulously and accurately and he liked to be in control. His obsessive character is evident in various ways. He was very superstitious about certain numbers and he collected quantities of antique statuettes. He was a compulsive smoker and found it impossible to stop, even when he was diagnosed as having oral cancer in 1923. It was not until he had a heart attack in 1930 that he finally gave up.

Freud had friendships throughout his life and they tended to be fairly intense, although he was also prone to quarrels and disagreements. Some of his friends developed theories that were thought of as being even more eccentric than Freud's. For example, his friend Wilhelm Fliess was obsessed with the numbers 23 and 28, and thought the nose was an important sexual organ. However, the friendship with Fliess was typical of Freud's personal relationships, in that the two men exchanged many ideas and Fliess acted as a useful critic and advisor to Freud.

Fliess thought the nose was an important sexual organ.

Among his other hobbies, Freud enjoyed playing cards with his friends, or going for long walks and looking for mushrooms. People often think of him as a stern patriarch, but in fact his children recalled plenty of happy days when he would stop working and take them on family outings. He did not buy many clothes, and is reported to have only ever had three suits, three sets of underwear and three pairs of shoes at a time. However, he was not mean and later in life he gave financial support to various friends and students. He enjoyed literature, but he was a great music lover, apart from opera. Following the diagnosis of cancer, Freud suffered many painful medical treatments and surgical operations. He continued to write for the remaining sixteen years of his life, mainly philosophical and cultural publications.

In 1938 the Germans occupied Austria, and Freud and his family fled to England. He died in London on 23 September 1939.

✳ ✳ ✳ ✳ SUMMARY ✳ ✳ ✳ ✳

● Freud is famous because he founded a new system of psychology that he called psychoanalysis.

● Freud's work largely concerns the unconscious.

● He said that we have many inner motives for our behaviour, and that these are mostly sexual.

● His work falls into four main phases:

1 Studies on the causes and treatment of neurosis.

2 Developing ideas about the sexual origins of neurosis.

3 Ideas about how the psyche develops from birth onwards – often called id psychology.

4 Theories about the whole personality and the ways in which people relate to others. This is known as ego psychology.

2 Freud's Early Work

FREUD'S MEDICAL TRAINING

Freud entered the University of Vienna in 1873 to study medicine. He did not finish until 1881, so the course took him three years longer than was normal. This was because he enjoyed research and his interest lay more in this direc-

KEYWORD

Histology: branch of anatomy dealing with the structure of tissues.

tion than in actually becoming a doctor. He specialized in **histology** as well as neurology. The mechanistic approach to science that Freud was taught emphasized that living things could be understood purely in terms of physics and chemistry. The scientific method involved systematically observing, measuring and experimenting. This suited Freud's orderly, methodical way of thinking.

SCIENTIFIC RESEARCH

After graduating as a doctor of medicine in 1881, Freud went on to work in the research laboratory at the university. This is where he was given an assignment to investigate the sex organs of eels, about which nothing was known at the time. He also studied the nervous system of lampreys (a kind of fish) and his first published article was on this subject. He wrote about twenty neurology papers between 1887 and 1897.

The mechanistic scientific view insisted that the mind of a human being and an animal, such as a frog, differed only in their complexity. Even ideas were held to be merely the result of a complicated neurological process. This deterministic view was to remain with Freud throughout his life. He believed that all psychological phenomena, even fantasies, feelings and so on, rigidly followed the principle of cause and effect.

Freud would have happily stayed in medical research, but he realized that he would not have enough money to support a wife and family. He decided that he would have to go into medical practice and spent the next three years gaining practical medical experience at Vienna General Hospital. In 1885, Freud was appointed as a lecturer in neuropathology at Vienna University. In the same year he wrote an essay about scientific psychology. He was already beginning to embark on his life-long quest to bridge the gap between the exact science of neurology and psychology.

HYSTERIA AND HYPNOSIS

The time that Freud spent working with Charcot in Paris was to have a profound effect upon his thinking. Charcot was working with cases of paralysis, trying to discover a way of distinguishing when they were the result of **organic disease** in the nervous system and when they were hysterical, or neurotic in origin.

KEYWORD

Organic disease: disease that relates to particular body structures or functions.

Doctors found hysteria interesting for several reasons.

* The symptoms were very varied. They included memory loss, hallucinations, loss of speech, sleepwalking, paralysis, fits and loss of sensation.

* Only women were supposed to suffer from it. In fact the word hysteria is derived from a Greek word *hustera,* meaning 'womb'. Charcot disagreed and said that men could have hysteria too.

* It baffled doctors because it did not fit in with the anatomy of the nervous system. For example, an arm might be paralysed right up to the shoulder, even though the nerves do not stop precisely there.

Charcot realized that a patient's own ideas could affect the area of the paralysis. A person's paralysis could stop at a neat line because the person *thought* that the limb began or ended at that line. Charcot discovered that this type of paralysis could be cured, or even induced, by hypnosis. This led Freud to two very important new ideas.

* To understand hysteria it is necessary to look at the patient's psychology, rather than just neurology.

* Unconscious mental processes can affect behaviour. Although a patient's behaviour could be affected by hypnosis, he or she often did not recall what had happened during the session.

Freud's new ideas may seem rather unstartling to us nowadays, but it is only recently that we have gained any understanding of mental illness. In the past, hysterics were persecuted, often locked up, or burnt as witches, because the unusual and sometimes frightening way they behaved was attributed to the presence of demons. Even Charcot thought that hysterics suffered from a genetic weakness in the brain – for him the cause of hysteria had to be purely physical, because he was a strict mechanist. He also thought that only hysterics could be hypnotized. Freud had other ideas and began to think about whether hypnosis could be used as a therapy.

Freud began his own private practice as a neuropathologist in 1886. Two main methods of treatment were currently in use with neurotic patients.

Electrotherapy
This involved local electrical stimulation of the skin and muscles. Freud considered this method to be useless and said that when it did seem to work it was only because of the power of suggestion. In other words he was once again stating that mental processes could affect physical symptoms.

Hypnosis
New research was beginning to suggest that this could work on 'normal' people too. Being susceptible to hypnosis was no longer regarded as a sign of brain damage or genetic weakness.

In 1886, Freud gave a lecture on male hysteria to the Vienna Society of Physicians. He was already being looked upon with scorn because of his interest in Charcot's ideas. This new outrage – the very idea that *men* could suffer from hysteria – met with a fresh wave of hostility. Freud began to realize that his ideas were always going to be unconventional and that he would have to get used to this type of reaction. It was certainly not to be the only occasion that his ideas were to be ridiculed.

The very idea that *men* could suffer from hysteria!

NINETEENTH-CENTURY SCIENTIFIC AND MORAL THINKING

It is very important to try and understand Freud's work within the context of the times in which he lived. It is easy to dismiss some of his ideas as ludicrous and obsessive. Prevailing views and ideas included the following.

* A mechanistic view of science, making it difficult to look at the way in which a person's mind and ideas can affect their behaviour.

* Great arguments between scientists and religious thinkers, stemming from the work of Charles Darwin.

* A prudish attitude towards sex, making it difficult to study or discuss anything sexual in a scientific way.

* A patriarchal system, in which men still tended to think they were naturally superior to women.

The mechanistic view

The normal way of thinking in science in Freud's day followed the rules of **positivism**. Positivism limits knowledge to things which are directly observable. This goes hand-in-hand with the mechanistic and deterministic approaches. The goal of this way of thinking is simple – you simply describe the facts of what you can experience and observe. Anything else is not science. Positivists try to make general scientific laws about the ways in which phenomena are related. This approach began in the natural sciences and spread into **philosophy**.

Freud struggled with trying to apply positivism to the way the mind worked. This proved to be tricky, because thoughts, feelings, fantasies and moods are **abstract** in their nature rather than concrete and are therefore hard to observe. Most psychologists took the positivist stance, but **psychiatry** was also developing, as people became interested in mental illnesses. It was hard to explain these illnesses by means of conventional medicine and mechanistic thinking.

KEYWORDS

Positivism: a way of thinking that limits knowledge to that which is directly observable.

Philosophy: a system of learning that investigates the underlying nature and truth of knowledge and existence.

Abstract: existing in thought rather than in solid matter.

Concrete: existing in a material form.

Psychiatry: the study and treatment of mental illnesses.

Charles Darwin

Darwin caused great uproar in the nineteenth-century with his revolutionary ideas about evolution. Darwin's theory of evolution said that the animals and plants that we see today had all descended from an original simple life form. This process depended on 'natural selection', whereby successful species tended to survive and could therefore hand on their genes. Accidental variations in the genes led to new species gradually evolving, while unsuccessful variations died out.

Darwin's ideas were a direct challenge to the traditional religious view that God had created all species fully formed from the beginning. Like Darwin, Freud challenged traditional thinking and met with great opposition.

Prudish attitudes to sex

Sex was almost totally unmentionable in the late nineteenth century. Freud himself said that it was something improper that one ought not to talk about it. In such an atmosphere it is hardly surprising that many of Freud's patients had sexual hang-ups.

Patriarchy

Some of Freud's ideas seem sexist today, but we have to remember that it was very much the norm for women to defer to men. The man was the undisputed boss within the family, and women tended to lead very restricted, boring lives. This, in combination with the strong taboos about sex, meant that women's psychology was as yet very poorly understood.

FREUD'S FIRST IDEAS ABOUT THE UNCONSCIOUS

During the 1890s Freud worked closely with a friend and colleague, Josef Breuer. Breuer told Freud about an interesting case history, the case of 'Anna O'. Anna was a young woman of 21 who suffered from a bewildering variety of symptoms. She had a nervous cough, speech problems, paralysis of her right arm and neck, and also had hallucinations. Her hallucinations would gradually get worse through the day until in the evening she fell into a strange trance. While in this state she would mumble odd words.

Anna had recently been nursing her father night and day until he died. This traumatic experience seemed to have triggered her illness. Breuer found that if he repeated her trance words then she would describe her hallucinations to him. This made her a little better for a brief time, but then fresh symptoms would seem to arise. Breuer discovered that when each symptom was traced back to its origin it would then disappear.

The origin of each symptom would turn out to be a forgotten traumatic event. While Anna was actually discussing the trauma her symptoms got very severe.

Breuer also used hypnosis to further insights into Anna's problems. His method of curing symptoms, by releasing suppressed traumatic memories, became known as the **cathartic method**. He stopped treating Anna when she became very dependent on him and fell in love with him. Anna was eventually able to lead a fulfilling life as a social worker and feminist. Her real name was Bertha Pappenheim.

In 1895, Freud and Breuer together published *Studies in Hysteria*. This work presented some rather radical new ideas.

KEYWORDS

Cathartic method: method of therapy involving the freeing of repressed emotions.

Repression: process of banishing unpleasant or undesirable feelings into the unconscious.

Affect: emotion attached to an idea.

Abreaction: release of repressed emotions.

* Negative mental processes can directly affect the physical body and lead to a diseased state. Any traumatic memory that is painful, frightening or shameful in some way can do this.

* Negative memories remain active in the unconscious mind and can alter our behaviour. We cannot get rid of them unless they are recalled, i.e. brought back into the conscious mind.

* The banishment of unpleasant memories to the unconscious requires an active process operating at an unconscious level. Freud called this process **repression**. Freud called repression the 'first mechanism of defence', and this idea is one of the cornerstones of psychoanalytic thinking.

* The repressed emotional energy, or **affect**, is converted into hysterical symptoms. These can be permanently erased by **abreaction**, when the original trauma is relived and gone over in detail.

* A symptom is often **overdetermined** which means that it is actually caused by several separate events. This makes therapy more difficult.

٭ Symptoms often prove to be symbolic – for example a pain in the heart area when a person had a 'broken heart'.

KEYWORDS

Overdetermined: when more than one root cause is present.

Resistance: process that prevents unconscious ideas from being released.

Freud soon found that some of his patients were resistant to all this unravelling, and he decided that the resistance was sexual in origin. Breuer disagreed with him and there was soon a parting of the ways. Freud slowly abandoned hypnotism and developed a new technique that was called the 'pressure technique'. The patient relaxed on a couch and the analyst pressed on his or her forehead, announcing that memories would now be recalled. This method made the analyst into a figure of authority.

Freud's work was gradually suggesting the existence of conflict between two parts of the mind. One part wanted to release a blocked-up emotion, but another part found the release unacceptable and refused to look at it. This conflict led to a process that Freud called **resistance**. It was ideas like this that gradually led Freud to his discoveries about the unconscious.

٭ ٭ ٭ ٭ *SUMMARY* ٭ ٭ ٭ ٭

● Freud trained originally in medicine.

● After working with Charcot in Paris he became interested in hysteria and hypnosis.

● Freud began his own private practice as a neuropathologist in 1886, using electrotherapy and hypnosis to treat patients.

● The commonly accepted scientific view at this time was the mechanistic view.

● Many of Freud's ideas were regarded with suspicion by other scientists.

● Freud became interested in the unconscious while working with Josef Breuer in Vienna.

3 The Beginnings of Psychoanalysis

THE REPRESSION OF SEXUAL IDEAS

Freud's theories about psychoanalysis had already begun to evolve during his time working with Breuer. The rift between the two friends came in 1894.

At first Freud thought that neurotic symptoms were always caused by traumatic events, but eventually case studies led him to the discovery that they can also be caused by repressed sexual urges. He saw the human psyche as constantly striving towards a peaceful state. This meant that any strong emotions, either positive or negative, were seen as unpleasant and therefore needed to be eradicated in order to release tension. This idea was later named the 'Nirvana principle'.

Freud now claimed confidently that *all* neurotic symptoms are caused by sexual experiences, often in early childhood. Sexual satisfaction was the key to happiness and emotional balance. This idea became central to psychoanalytic theory, and Freud remained obstinately adamant about it for a long time. However, we must remember the times in which Freud lived and the prevailing attitudes towards sex. Moreover, there was no proper means of birth control. This meant that once your family was complete, you had to abstain, or furtively seek satisfaction elsewhere.

THE SEDUCTION THEORY

As a result of early case studies Freud focused more and more on the influence of sexual experience. He claimed that the key to all neuroses was in fact the suppressed memory of an early childhood seduction by an adult. This experience only led to a neurosis if it was suppressed. It then festered in the unconscious, only to re-emerge at puberty as a neurosis.

After a while Freud abandoned this theory, for several reasons. The whole picture was suspiciously common – could it be that some of his patients were inventing the whole thing to fit in with their doctor's theory? Furthermore, some of his own siblings showed neurotic symptoms – surely his own father was not guilty of incest? Freud now had a better idea, and argued that some of the 'memories' were in fact fantasies that arose in order to fulfil hidden desires.

This was an important breakthrough – it had dawned on Freud that fantasies could actually be more important than real events in our struggle to understand the human psyche. People had fantasies that were based on instinctive urges. This gradually led Freud to develop his theories about infantile sexuality and dreams. Until then people had tended to think that children were totally devoid of sexual urges. Once again Freud was producing new and uncomfortable ideas.

THE FREE ASSOCIATION TECHNIQUE

Freud gradually began to realize that there was a snag with both hypnosis and the pressure method that he had been using to help his

You *will* remember.

patients. In both cases the analyst was put in a position of authority and the client was not in control. Using the pressure method also meant that the analyst's voice could interrupt the patient's flow of thought. Even worse, he recognized a tendency for the analyst actually to plant ideas that might not have been there to begin with.

Freud therefore developed a modified version of the pressure technique. The patient was encouraged to relax on the couch and then simply feel free to voice whatever thought drifted into his or her mind. The role of the analyst had now changed – ideally he or she was there simply to guide the patient, although in practice it was not always easy to retain this passive role. This new method was called the **free association technique**. The idea behind it was that only the patient could really discover the key to the neurosis – this method put the patient back in control of what went on. However, Freud discovered that when the patient got close to the root cause of the neurosis, resistance was likely to occur.

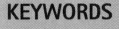

KEYWORDS

Free association technique: method used in psycho-analysis where the patient is encouraged to say whatever he or she feels, without censorship.

Transference: emotional attitudes developed by the patient towards the analyst.

From 1894 until 1900 Freud developed many of the theories that we now see as being central to psychoanalysis. He carefully examined and analysed the unconscious mechanisms, such as repression and resistance, that he saw underlying neurotic symptoms. He also became interested in **transference**. 'Transference' was a word he used to describe the emotional feelings that the client developed towards the analyst. This could involve either positive or negative emotions. For example the client may actually fall in love with the therapist, as Anna O did with Breuer. Alternatively the client might become very hostile towards the analyst.

Freud coined the term 'psychoanalysis' in 1896. The main theories that he was developing during this period were connected with:

* dream analysis;
* slips of speech;
* infantile sexuality.

FREUD'S SELF-ANALYSIS

In 1896, Freud's father died. For the next three years Freud went through a period of gloom, while he struggled to come to terms with conflicting feelings thrown up by his father's death. On the one hand he felt love and respect towards his father, and on the other he felt hostility and guilt. Freud had many responsibilities by this time. He had six children, and his wife, mother and some of his sisters were all dependent on him too. His father's death must have left him feeling very alone in the world. This experience reinforced Freud's belief in the huge importance of the male as the figurehead of the family.

However, his period of darkness (one that we now regard as common when we reach middle age) did have its plus side. This was because it threw him into a period of intensive self-analysis that was to prove very productive. He began to realize that he had long repressed feelings of resentment and rage towards his father and that these emotions were now emerging in the form of feelings of shame and impotence. This revelation led him to examine his childhood memories and his dreams.

Freud realized that unconscious childhood memories often surfaced in adult dreams. For example, he recalled having had sexual feelings towards his mother when he caught sight of her naked when he was a child. The importance of repressed childhood memories, which emerge in dreams and fantasies, became central to psychoanalytic theory.

During his period of self-analysis Freud wrote *The Interpretation of Dreams*. This book contains analyses of many of Freud's own dreams. He was as objective as possible when working with his own dreams, trying to view himself as he would a client. By the time the book was published in 1900 he was much more confident about his theories and had laid down the main foundations of psychoanalytic thinking. He was using two main approaches with his clients, and these are still used today.

The free association method

Freud encouraged his patients to make connections between mental images and hidden memories. By talking about these he found that he could lead the person deeper and deeper into the unconscious.

Dream analysis

Freud found that dreams were a very revealing way of accessing what lay in the unconscious.

A second important book, *Psychopathology of Everyday Life*, also appeared at the end of Freud's period of withdrawal, in 1901. This book deals with what have become known as Freudian slips of speech and similar mistakes in speech and writing (see Chapter 5).

THE ANALYSIS OF DORA

Dora was an eighteen-year-old girl whom Freud saw as a client in 1900. The case is interesting for two reasons. Firstly, it is one of the earliest recorded case histories in psychoanalysis and one of the first where dreams were used as the main basis for the analysis. Although the therapy itself was a failure the case was used for years as a classic case study for students. Secondly, it highlights some possible pitfalls in the psychoanalytic method.

Dora's father had already been to Freud as a patient, and he brought Dora to see Freud in order to see if he could help her as well. (An interesting statement that may give a clue about the real source of Dora's neurosis!) She displayed typical hysterical symptoms, such as fainting, depression and losing her voice. By the time she came to see Freud she had also threatened suicide.

The story is a complicated one, but the main point was that Dora had a crush on Frau K, who was her father's mistress. Meanwhile Frau K's husband, Herr K, had allegedly made sexual advances to Dora since she was 14. A tangled web indeed. Dora vehemently and consistently announced that she hated Herr K, but Freud interpreted this as meaning that the root of the problem was that she was secretly in love with him. The more Dora declared her hatred, the more Freud announced that this was clear evidence of repression of her true feelings – Heads I win, tails you lose.

Eventually, after eleven weeks in therapy, Dora quit. By now she had been labelled a lesbian, and the analysis certainly did nothing to alter her sexual orientation. However, Freud claimed that she had eventually accepted the idea that she was in love with Herr K. This perhaps illustrates how pig-headed and persuasive Freud could be once he got the bit between his teeth!

Dora finally accepts the idea that she is in love with Herr K.

✳ ✳ ✳ ✳ SUMMARY ✳ ✳ ✳ ✳

- Early on in the development of psychoanalysis, Freud decided that all neurotic symptoms were caused by sexual experiences.

- At first he claimed that the key to all neuroses was in fact the suppressed memory of an early childhood seduction by an adult.

- He developed a new therapeutic technique called the free association technique. He used mainly free association and dream analysis in his therapy.

- Freud coined the term 'psychoanalysis' in 1896.

- The analysis of 'Dora' is one of the earliest recorded case histories in psychoanalysis.

The Interpretation of Dreams

WHY DREAMS ARE IMPORTANT IN PSYCHOANALYSIS

Freud was very interested in dreams and emphasized their importance in psychoanalysis. In fact, dream analysis and free association became the two main therapeutic methods in psychoanalysis.

Dreams are central to psychoanalysis for several reasons.

* They occur during sleep, when the conscious mind releases its hold and is 'off guard'. Freud saw dreams as evidence of the unconscious mind at work and proof of its existence. He referred to dreams as being the 'royal road' to deeper understanding of the unconscious.

* Freud had come to realize that hypnosis and the pressure method were too authoritarian. He realized that you cannot force a person to understand what is going on in their unconscious. Only by the new methods of dream analysis and free association could symbolism involved in neurotic symptoms really be understood.

* While Freud was busy working out his main theories about dreams, he was also developing ideas about infantile sexuality. He emphasized that dreams are often concerned with sexual issues from very early childhood, and that problems could only be resolved through dream analysis and free association.

* Freud saw all dreams as expressions of wish fulfilment. By exploring the hidden desire symbolized in a dream it was possible to begin to unravel the problem.

DREAMS AS WISH FULFILMENT

It is common today for people to see dreams as wish fulfilment fantasies. We use phrases like 'in your dreams' or 'not even in my wildest dreams'. Freud claimed that dreams were *always* driven by the need to fulfil a wish. In its simplest form, a dream directly expresses a wish. For example, Freud describes the dream of a young mother who was cut off from society for weeks while she nursed a child through an infectious illness. In her dream she met lots of well-known authors and had fascinating conversations with them. Similarly, when Freud's daughter Anna was sick and not allowed any food, she dreamt of strawberries, omelette and pudding. This type of direct wish fulfilment dream is common in small children.

Strawberries, omelette and pudding.

Freud saw dreaming as a form of regression to childhood and the instinctual forces and images that dominate this time of our lives. He believed that recent events and desires played a minor role in dreams. In this respect Freud's ideas differ from other modern theories about dreams where recent and current events are regarded as very important. Freud argued that wishes represented in dreams must be infantile desires. He admitted that this was not invariably the case, but insisted that it was usually true, even when the infantile desire is not at first suspected.

In cases where it seemed impossible to unravel a hidden wish fulfilment, Freud cunningly used two possible explanations.

* The patient is in a state of negative transference to the analyst (see Chapter 8) and is deliberately producing awkward dreams in order to trip him or her up. To back this up, Freud cites a case where a barrister friend dreamed that he had lost all his cases. Freud and he had been rivals at school and Freud had always beaten him. Therefore he is identifying with Freud in the dream and hoping that *he* will lose. This means that the dream conceals a hidden wish fulfilment.

* The patient is employing mental masochism and the dream is satisfying a masochistic urge, which is in itself a form of wish fulfilment.

These explanations could perhaps be seen as further examples of Freud's own stubbornness when he wanted to prove a theory!

During and after World War I, Freud had experience with shock and trauma victims. They often relived recent ghastly war-time experiences in their dreams. This led Freud to question his insistence that dreams were always wish fulfilment and that they always harked back to childhood.

DREAM MECHANISMS

While it might be obvious that the simple type of dream can be a wish fulfilment fantasy, can the same be said of a nightmare or an anxiety dream? Freud explained this by saying that each dream has both a **manifest** and a **latent** content. If the dream is properly interpreted, a hidden wish fulfilment can still be found lurking beneath the apparent meaning of the dream.

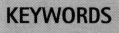

KEYWORDS

Manifest: the part of a dream that is consciously remembered.

Latent: the part of a dream that is not consciously remembered before analysis.

The latent content of the dream is actually the cause of the dream. Freud proposed two mechanisms at work here.

* The sleeping mind begins to create a dream, based on a wish fulfilment.

* The mind is shocked by the wish and imposes censorship on it. This causes distortion in the way the wish is allowed to appear in the dream.

Freud gives an example of this process. A patient of his dreamed that she wanted to hold a supper party, but various things kept going wrong: there was not enough food; it was Sunday, so she could not order more to be delivered; the phone was out of order... and so on. Analysis of the dream revealed a hidden jealousy of the friend whom she had been going to invite to the supper party. She was afraid that her husband was attracted to her friend, but fortunately the friend was skinny, and as her husband preferred plump women she felt reasonably safe. However, she was damned if she wanted to fatten her up with a special supper party!

Her husband preferred plump women.

Freud said that the latent content of the dream could only be revealed through dream analysis and free association. The latent aspect of the dream is seen as being the important part because it contains the real meaning, which has been censored. The thought processes of the unconscious brain are irrational and incomplete. The goal is simply to evade the censor and allow the dream ideas to be expressed somehow.

Freud suggested that there were various mechanisms at work, which allowed the dream wish to be expressed, but in a distorted form.

Displacement

Feelings about a situation are not expressed directly, but are associated in the dream with something different. The manifest content of the dream is very different from the latent content, but the feelings themselves remain very much the same.

Condensation

Two or more ideas are fused together in the dream. In this way a dream image may have more than one root cause. Much deeper real meanings may lie behind the dream image.

KEYWORDS

Displacement: shifting of emotions attached to one idea onto a different idea.

Condensation: fusion of two or more ideas – in a dream or in telling a joke.

Symbolization: representing an object or idea by a different object or idea.

Symbolization

Dream images or ideas are often symbolic, so that they secretly represent other things. According to Freud, most dream symbolism is sexual in nature.

Resistance

Freud said that we tend to forget dreams because of dream censorship, which still tries to prevent the dream ideas from entering conscious thought.

METHODS OF DREAM INTERPRETATION

Freud maintained that every dream has a meaning. He realized that this was not a new idea – even the Greek philosopher Aristotle (384–322 BC) saw dreams not as sent by the gods, but as the mental activity of the sleeper. The prevailing mechanistic view of Freud's time tended to lead people to see dreams as being the meaningless result of physical processes in the sleeping body. Freud disagreed, pointing out that dreams have been viewed throughout history as being full of hidden meaning. He described two ways in which dreams were usually interpreted.

* **The symbolic method**: in Joseph's dream in the Bible, seven fat cows are followed by seven thin cows that eat them up. This was interpreted symbolically as meaning that seven years of famine would follow seven years of plenty. This method tended not to work where dreams were very confused and unintelligible.

* **The decoding method**: here a fixed key was used to interpret the meaning of the dream. Freud said that this method was not scientific because the original key could be wrong.

Freud discovered that while his patients were relaxing and free associating ideas they began to tell him about their dreams. He saw their dreams as further symptoms, and the method he used to unravel them was really the same free association method as he used for other problems. During the process of free association and dream analysis the patient had to feel relaxed and safe. This meant that two things could happen.

* The patient and analyst could both pay closer attention to what was going on in the patient's thought processes.

* They were able to remove the critical censor that normally sifts thought processes as they arise.

In effect, Freud's new method was reversing the critical, repressive attitudes that prevailed in Vienna at the time. He was encouraging people to look at themselves in an uncritical way. Freud helped people to analyse each part of a dream separately often a painstaking process. In his book *The Interpretation of Dreams* he analyses many of his own dreams because he felt that his clients, being 'neuropaths', might have dreams that did not represent the 'norm'. Also, to analyse clients' dreams would often mean exposing a good deal of confidential case history.

Freud gave advice about dream interpretation that is still very helpful today.

* To interpret a dream is hard work and requires perseverance.

* After working on a dream it should then be left alone – fresh insights may come later.

* Dreams often occur in groups with a common underlying theme. An insight into one dream may unravel a whole series of dreams.

* Something that seems trivial or superficial in a dream may actually be masking a deep insight.

* It is important for the analyst to pay attention to all the client's remarks, however trivial they may seem on the surface.

FREUDIAN SYMBOLS

Freud believed that much of a dream's content was disguised by means of symbols. Freudian symbols within dreams have become one of the most well-known aspects of psychoanalytic thinking. Freud believed that symbols frequently have more than one meaning and that correct interpretation can only be arrived at by analysing the dream. To understand symbols he used a combination of two methods:

* exploration of the dreamer's own associations;

* using the analyst's knowledge of common dream symbols to fill in the gaps.

Freud's own ideas about what symbols mean are notoriously sexual. For example, he suggested the following interpretations.

* Sticks, knives, umbrellas, and other pointy objects represent the penis.

* Boxes, chests, ovens, cupboards and other containers represent the uterus.

* Movement up and down ladders, stairs, seesaws etc. represents having sex.

* Playing with a little child represents masturbation.

However, Freud warned that it was not always easy or straightforward to find the correct interpretation of a dream symbol.

ORIGINS OF DREAMS

Freud noticed that a good deal of dream content came from recent events or emotional reactions. He explained that often these were actually distortions, masking deeper emotional issues that were connected to the recent events by long trains of association. In the same way, he maintained that childhood memories were also linked to recent events by associations. Thus the dream is often not really about current affairs at all.

Although dreams often appear to be trivial, Freud maintained that all dreams were significant because of their latent content. The significance of some dreams was immediately obvious, whereas others needed to be unravelled through analysis before their importance could be appreciated. Often several ideas converged to form a dream image by the condensation process.

＊＊＊＊SUMMARY＊＊＊＊

- Dreams are of central importance in psychoanalysis.

- Freud saw dreams as wish fulfilments.

- He said that each dream has both a manifest and a latent content.

- He identified special mechanisms that prevented the latent content from becoming conscious.

- Freud believed that much of a dream's content was disguised by means of symbols.

- He maintained that most dreams harked back to childhood experiences.

Exploring the Unconscious 5

Freud gradually became interested in extending psychoanalytic exploration to try and discover how the 'normal' human mind operates. This step was important because it meant that psychoanalysis was no longer limited to abnormal psychology. Freud gradually discovered that the unconscious plays a huge part in determining the behaviour of all of us. This means that his ideas have become important to ordinary people as well as psychiatrists and analysts, so that Freud himself has become more widely known as a result.

THE DIVISIONS OF THE MIND

To begin with Freud decided that there were two states of consciousness.

The conscious mind

This is the part of the mind that is aware of its thoughts and actions. It is where all conscious thought processes occur, and is the source of ideas and understanding. It is concerned with logical thinking, reality and civilized behaviour.

The unconscious

This is the part of the mind that is repressed, the place where we put anything that our conditioning does not allow us to look at. Information in the unconscious cannot easily be accessed. Much of our past history lies here too, some of which can only be recalled under hypnosis.

Eventually, Freud concluded that this simple division was not completely accurate. He proposed the existence of a third level of consciousness, the **preconscious** where information is stored that is not conscious at the moment, but can easily be recalled when needed.

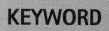

KEYWORD

Preconscious: the region of the mind between conscious and unconscious, where material is stored away but readily accessible.

Imagine the psyche as a house. The conscious mind is the living quarters, while the preconscious is a filing cabinet where information is stored ready for reference. The unconscious is the cellar, or perhaps a loft, where you need a ladder to get in.

THE PLEASURE PRINCIPLE AND THE REALITY PRINCIPLE

Freud suggested two opposing processes that control normal human behaviour.

The pleasure principle

This pushes people towards immediate gratification of wishes. It is the tendency behind all natural impulses and basic urges. It is linked to the unconscious and is impulsive, primitive and disorganized. According to Freud, it governs us right from birth and is basically to do with the gratification of sexual urges – Freud did not seem to consider other drives, such as hunger, when he was talking about this drive. The pleasure principle is always the main motive force of the unconscious.

The reality principle

As a person matures and has to operate in a social environment, the opposing force, which is called the reality principle, comes into play. It involves conscious, logical thinking, and it allows us to delay gratification in order to get on with everyday life.

Freud used the word **libido** to describe the sexual drive, which he claimed was the driving force for most behaviour. The reality principle causes libidinal energy (sexual energy) to be redirected into safer or more socially acceptable behaviour. This unconscious redirection is called **sublimation**.

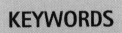

KEYWORDS

Libido: sexual drive.

Sublimation: unconscious process by which libido is transferred to a non-sexual, socially acceptable or safe activity.

According to Freud psychic conflicts arise as a result of the conflict between sexual drive (ruled by the pleasure principle) and survival (ruled by the reality principle). After a while, however, he changed his mind about the two forces being in opposition. He decided that they actually worked together, because both led to a decrease in tension. This decrease in tension was held to be the purpose of all behaviour.

Freud was often criticized for modifying his ideas in this kind of way. He found this criticism annoying and pointed out that by changing their views, scientists are often seen as fickle and unreliable, yet by not changing their views, they are seen as obstinate and pig-headed. He claimed it was tiresome to be criticised for holding views that had been modified long ago.

It seems typical of Freud's pessimistic outlook on life that the 'pleasure principle' is actually all about avoiding pain! It is not about pleasures such as love, joy, fun and friendship. Freud always tended to view any powerful emotion as negative, as something that needed to be expelled in order for a person to feel comfortable. According to Freud, a person's character is determined by the way libido is channelled into more acceptable activity. If libido is blocked up without an outlet, then neuroses or other psychological problems develop. Psychoanalysis is all about finding out what urges have been blocked up and why.

After a while Freud discovered a snag with the idea of the pleasure principle. He found that patients who suffered from neuroses caused by trauma tended to keep on endlessly acting out the original scene in their imagination. Small children also do this in a more concrete way, by actually acting out nasty experiences. This probably gives them some sense of control over the incident. Freud eventually began to evolve a new theory about the 'death instinct' as an attempt to deal with this problem.

PARAPRAXIS

Parapraxis (plural 'parapraxes') is Freud's term for the now famous 'Freudian slip'. Freud became interested in parapraxes because they occurred frequently in the lives of perfectly 'normal' people, and seemed to him to demonstrate that the unconscious was at work.

KEYWORD

Parapraxis: general term for a 'Freudian slip', i.e. a slip of the tongue, or forgetting someone's name.

His popular book *Psychopathology of Everyday Life* is all about parapraxes. The title of the book is interesting in itself, because the word **psychopathology** implies that Freud believed parapraxes to be symptoms of abnormality or disorder, despite their universal occurrence.

KEYWORD

Psychopathology: the study of abnormal mental processes.

Freud identified a whole list of different forms of parapraxis:

* forgetting peoples' names;
* forgetting something one intended to do;
* slips of the tongue, or pen;
* misreading or mishearing;
* losing or temporarily mislaying things;
* bungled actions and accidents;
* remembering things wrongly.

Freud claimed that none of these are actually innocent accidental mistakes. They all reveal the unconscious at work on a cover-up job again, rather like the dreaming process. Thoughts that are painful or socially unacceptable are disguised by means of a Freudian slip. The slip is seen not as a silly, chance mistake, but as a subconscious mental act.

Slips of speech are often caused by the influence of something that is connected to the misspoken word by a chain of thought. Sometimes they occur when the person anticipates a taboo word coming up, or perhaps feels that the conversation is getting uncomfortably close to revealing his or her true feelings. In fact, any kind of parapraxis arises as a result of two different intentions in a person's mind that are acting in opposition. They reveal what the person is *really* thinking. According to Freud all parapraxes occur in this way and if they are analysed this will nearly always prove to be the case. However, it is not possible to actually prove that his theory is true. Other psychologists argued that parapraxes are caused by factors such as fatigue, excitement or distraction. Freud admitted that this was true, but insisted that such an explanation missed the point – such conditions simply make it easier or more likely for slips to occur. Freud could be clever and persuasive when he wanted to argue a point.

Some examples of parapraxis
Forgetting proper names

Freud gives an example of this where, try as he might, he could not recall a place name. In the end he had to ask his wife and daughter for help. They were amused, saying that of course he would forget a name like that – the place was called Nervi. Freud had quite enough to do with nerves in his daily work, and so had pushed the name out of his mind. Very often a wrong proper name will intrude in place of the correct one. When this occurs the two are usually connected by a train of associations. The subconscious wants to forget the name because it has painful or embarrassing associations. Or it may just be connected with a topic one has had enough of, such as work as in the example given by Freud.

Parapraxis in action.

Interestingly, Freud points out that name forgetting is very contagious. If one person has difficulty recalling a name, it is common for a friend to struggle with it too.

Forgetting childhood memories

Many childhood memories are not consciously recalled by the adult. Freud observed that children frequently remembered trivial events rather than important ones. He says that both these facts indicate a process of displacement going on – the child substitutes a trivial memory in order to conceal a painful one. Freud calls this type of memory a 'concealing memory', and says that they form a large part of our total memory bank. He seems to overlook the possibility that sometimes children might seem to remember trivia because, for them, those are the things that have assumed importance.

Accidents

Even accidents, such as tripping over, are parapraxes. Freud says that they show unconscious feelings being expressed in a physical way. We all know examples of people who seem to get themselves injured almost on purpose in order to be able to lap up attention. Conversely we sometimes 'accidentally' hurt another person when we feel hostile towards them, or we may break an object such as a hideous vase because of a subconscious desire to get rid of it.

Freud gives various examples of 'bungled actions'. For example, Freud forbade one of his patients to contact a girl with whom he was madly in love. The patient accidentally used her telephone number instead when he was trying to contact Freud. This shows that bungled actions, like other errors, are often used to fulfil wishes that a person is consciously trying to deny.

Slips of the tongue

These are very common and can often be amusing in everyday conversation, e.g. 'he entrusted his money to a savings crank'. This category also includes spoonerisms, where bits of words are displaced, e.g. 'the student had tasted the whole worm'. The slip of the tongue can often be seen to be transparently covering up what the person would really like to have said.

Forgetting foreign words

Freud said that we are less likely to forget a word completely in our native language – a slip is more likely to appear instead. He goes on at great length about an occasion when he was trying to remember the name of an artist called Signorelli. He kept getting Botticelli or Boltraffio in his mind instead. His explanation for this covers about six pages in *Psychopathology of Everyday Life.* and involves a complicated diagram with such labels as 'death and sexuality' and 'repressed thoughts'. It is all very interesting and ingenious, but somehow the arrangement seems rather unlikely. Is the unconscious really that desperate to conceal fairly trivial thoughts? And how does it work out such a complex series of connections so quickly? The problem with this type of analysis is that it relies mainly on the free association process. This method usually leads quite rapidly to the uncovering of supposedly 'significant material', even if you start with an innocent, neutral word.

Slips of the pen

Slips of the pen, like slips of the tongue, are common and easily recorded. Freud tells of an incident when he came home from holiday in September, and on starting work wrote the date as 'October 20th'. The explanation was that he was experiencing a lull in his work after the holiday period and had a client booked in to see him on the October date. So the slip was a kind of wish fulfilment process, wishing that the date would hurry up and arrive.

JOKES AND THE UNCONSCIOUS

Freud was also interested in the way jokes demonstrate the workings of the unconscious. His book, *Jokes and Their Relation to the Unconscious* appeared in 1905. It is quite a collection of jokes, mainly Jewish ones (unfortunately, many of the jokes recorded here do not come across very well in translation). The main point he made was that some of the mechanisms used in jokes are the same as those used in dreams. For example, one word is substituted for another, or condensation is used. He claimed once again that repression and sublimation of unconscious material is taking place.

Freud identified two categories of jokes.

* **Tendentious jokes**: this type is dependent on indirect expression of hostility or sexual urges. The category would include the classic mother-in-law joke, and the dirty joke.

* **Innocent jokes**: these depend on verbal ingenuity. The category would include puns and riddles.

The first category is the one in which Freud was chiefly interested. Such jokes allow the joker to get around internal inhibition by expressing an urge indirectly. For example, schoolboy humour often involves rude jokes which are told to relieve adolescent tension. The urge being indirectly expressed may be either sexual or aggressive. Freud eventually claimed that *all* jokes are in fact tendentious, the innocent ones being a kind of foreplay leading up to the tendentious ones! Freud had a tendency to reduce everything to the need to release libidinal tension and the chief criticism of his work on jokes is that he overlooks fun, wit, clever word-play, and the cathartic effect of simply having a good laugh among friends.

All Freud's work on dreams, the pleasure and reality principles and parapraxes is actually looking at ways in which the ego *defends* itself. If the ego finds an idea too painful or embarrassing or socially unaccept-able then the idea is repressed. The unconscious then finds endless little ways of letting the ideas leak back out.

* * * *SUMMARY* * * *

* Freud divided the mind into three sections – the conscious, preconscious and unconscious.

* He suggested two opposing processes that controlled human behaviour. These were the pleasure principle and the reality principle.

* Psychic conflicts arise as a result of conflict between the two processes.

* Freud was interested in parapraxes and jokes because they showed the unconscious at work in normal people.

Sexual Theories

Theories about sexuality and sexual development became important in psychoanalysis from an early stage. Freud published his book *Three Essays on Sexuality* in 1905. He explained that it was difficult to define exactly what was meant by the word 'sexual'. To say that it meant everything to do with the differences between the two sexes was too vague. On the other hand, the view that it was only concerned with actual genital contact between two people of the opposite sex, was too limiting. This meant that sex was only connected with what Freud saw as being 'improper'. Furthermore, to say that it meant everything to do with reproduction would leave out obviously sexual things such as kissing and masturbation. Freud concluded that the word 'sexual' concerned *all* these things and more.

FREUD ATTACKS CURRENT THINKING

The acceptable view of sex during Freud's time was that it involved bringing the genitals into contact with those of somebody of the opposite sex, and that this naturally entailed kissing, looking at and touching the other person. This behaviour did not surface until puberty, when the body became sexually mature, and was only concerned with reproduction. Freud caused uproar when he suggested that people needed to take a much broader view in order to study sex scientifically. He pointed out the following.

* Homosexual people are often only attracted sexually to members of their own sex. They may even find the opposite sex repellent. Freud called this group of people 'inverts'. For them sexuality has nothing to do with the reproductive process.

* For other people the sexual drive disregards the genitals or their normal use. They may be turned on by inappropriate body parts, inanimate objects, and so on. Freud said that the words 'sexual' and 'genital' therefore had very different meanings. Freud calls this group of people 'perverts'.

* Psychoanalytical research had shown that neurotic problems and perversions were often caused by early childhood sexual experiences. As children were not supposed to have a sex life, this suggestion caused particular furore.

What Freud was really doing was extending the concept of what was 'sexual'. He did this in order to support his theory that neuroses were caused by sexual problems and that neurotic symptoms therefore had sexual meaning. He found that neurotics often showed great resistance to any mention of sex. Their sexual urges were often very strongly repressed. Normal people on the other hand, satisfied their sexual urges in ordinary sexual activity and in dreams.

SEXUAL DEVIATIONS

Freud defines various types of sexual deviations, which he divides into two groups:

* deviations in respect of the **sexual object**;
* deviations in respect of the **sexual aim**.

This division seems rather artificial, and even Freud tends to get muddled about it, saying for example, that fetishism could go into either category.

> # KEYWORDS
>
> Sexual object: person or thing from which the sexual attraction comes.
>
> Sexual aim: the sexual act that a person is driven towards.

Inversion

This is the word Freud uses for homosexuality. He recognizes different types of behaviour in this category.

* Some people are attracted exclusively to their own sex.
* Some are attracted to both sexes.
* Some people turn to their own sex when the need arises, e.g. in prison.

Freud goes on to say that some inverts accept their sexuality as a natural state of affairs, whereas others are horrified by it and see it as a pathological compulsion. In the more extreme cases the person has been an invert from a very early age and is more likely to have accepted the state of affairs.

Freud was not able to identify one single sexual aim among inverts. Nor was it possible to find a satisfactory explanation for the origin of inversion. But he did say that it points us to one important fact – that the sexual instinct does not always draw us to the same object. In fact, it is surprisingly common for deviations to occur.

Oral and anal sex

Oral and anal sex were considered perversions by Freud. He said that a feeling of disgust prevents most people from indulging in either perversion. This is one of the natural repressive mechanisms that make people develop in the direction of 'normal' sexuality. However, the repression can be so forceful that the genitals of the opposite sex seem totally disgusting too. Freud found this to be a common reaction among hysterics.

Fetishism

Fetishism occurs when the normal sexual object becomes replaced by an object that bears some relation to it. The fetish object is usually non-sexual. For example it might be a different part of the body, such as the hair, or the feet, or it could be an inanimate object, such as an item of clothing. Freud said that fetishism usually occurred as the result of a sexual experience in early childhood, and a symbolic train of thought later connects the fetish to the sexual urge.

Touching and looking

Freud regarded tactile and visual stimulation between sexual partners as perfectly 'normal'. They only constituted a perversion if:

* they were restricted only to the genitals;
* they involved the overcoming of disgust – for example, in voyeurism, or in people who enjoy watching excretory functions;
* they totally supplanted the normal sexual aim.

Sadism and masochism

Sadism means the desire to inflict pain on the sexual object. Masochism is the desire to receive pain from the sexual object. Freud said that the roots of these two perversions are easy to detect. Male sexuality often has a strong element of aggression – there is the desire to overcome resistance and dominate the sexual partner. In sadism this urge gets out of hand. Masochism seemed rather further removed from the normal sexual aim. Freud said that it was probably caused primarily through guilt and fear. He saw it as a kind of extension of sadism, turned in upon the self. Freud said that there was definitely a connection between cruelty and the sexual instinct, but he was not able to explain why.

Freud drew several conclusions from his study of sexual deviations.

* The sexual instinct has to struggle against various mental resistances. This is probably a mechanism to keep the sexual instinct restrained within what is considered to be 'normal'.

* Some perversions are complex in their origin. This shows that the sexual instinct is a lot more complicated than people had previously maintained.

* The sexuality of neurotics has usually remained in, or been brought back to, an infantile state. This discovery brought Freud to the study of infantile sexuality.

INFANTILE SEXUALITY

The popular view in Freud's day was that sexuality lay dormant until puberty. Psychologists writing about child development generally omitted any reference to sexuality. To imply that *children* thought about sex was the ultimate horror. Once again, Freud stuck his neck out. He suggested two main reasons for the silence about infant sexuality:

* sex was a taboo subject;

* most people tend to forget what happens to them in early life until they reach the age of six to eight years.

Freud thought that this second aspect was strange, because small children show plenty of evidence of awareness and insight. However, early recollections could be brought to light under hypnosis. Freud therefore proposed that there was a special process of infantile **amnesia** that went into action to repress thoughts about sexual experiences.

KEYWORDS

Amnesia: an inability to remember, either total or partial.

Erotogenic zone: an area of the body where certain stimuli, especially rubbing, produce feelings of pleasure.

Latency period: period of development when sexual activity is dormant.

He claimed that sexual impulses are present from birth, but are soon overcome by a progressive process of repression. This process comes about as the child discovers that it has to comply with various rules in order to fit into society. Feelings of disgust and shame begin to arise and these suppress the sexual urge. The process of infantile amnesia is the forerunner of, and basis for, the process of hysterical amnesia in adult life.

According to Freud, infantile sexuality is not concerned only with the genital region. It shows up at different stages of development in various parts of the body, such as the oral zone, the anal zone and, finally, the genital zone. The aim of all infantile sexual activity is to get satisfaction by stimulating an **erotogenic zone**. After a while, at about age six to eight, this early sexual activity returns to a dormant state until puberty. This is known as the **latency period**.

Infant exploration of sexuality

Children are naturally curious about sex. Freud says that they explore sexuality in various ways.

They want to know where babies come from. Many of them are dissatisfied by nursery explanations such as the stork fetching them. Misunderstandings are common too, for example children may think the baby is born through the anus, because they are used to the idea of faeces appearing in this way.

Children are also curious to find out about the opposite sex. There was not so much scope for this in Freud's day, because children were kept 'decently' covered up. The eventual revelation was often very traumatic according to Freud. For boys it led to what Freud termed castration complex in which, having observed that the little girl had no penis, the boy was terrified that he would somehow lose his own. For girls it led to a terrible penis envy in which the little girl was overcome with jealousy at the male organ and she would immediately start wanting to be a boy.

Freud also claimed that if a child witnessed adults having sex, they invariably thought that they were fighting. Glimpses of menstrual blood on sheets or underwear only served to confirm this horrid suspicion.

THE STRUGGLES OF PUBERTY

Sexual changes in the physical body begin to occur at puberty and change the whole pattern of infantile sexuality. The early development can be described as three stages.

* The child's first sexual feelings arise from sucking at the mother's breast. At this very early stage the mother is the sexual object.

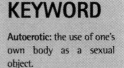

KEYWORD

Autoerotic: the use of one's own body as a sexual object.

* Next comes the stage of infantile sexuality where the child is excited by the sensations in its own body. This stage is **autoerotic** – the infant derives pleasure from its own body, so the child's own body is the sexual object.

* At puberty the child begins to be attracted to members of the opposite sex. A new sexual object has to be discovered.

At this point the two sexes diverge, because different functions emerge for their sexual aims. According to Freud the development of inhibitions of sexuality occurs earlier in little girls. He views the early auto-erotic and masturbatory activity of the infant as being 'wholly masculine' in both sexes. In little girls the erotogenic zone is the clitoris, which is **homologous** to the glans penis.

At puberty the sexual organs grow and begin to
work. This causes new sexual tensions. In boys
there is a great increase in libido, and this is fairly straightforward. But the unfortunate girls are
attacked by a fresh wave of suppression because
they have to overcome their previous masculine
sexuality and transfer the erotogenic zone from
the clitoris to the vagina. This process is very
difficult, and is a frequent cause of neurosis, especially hysteria.

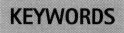

KEYWORDS

Homologous: fundamen-
tally similar in structure
and development.

Fixation getting stuck at a
particular stage in sexual
development.

Freud's theories on female sexuality and development now seem highly dubious. However, it is important to remember that he developed
these ideas nearly a hundred years ago, when female sexuality was very
poorly understood. Astoundingly, the true structure and function of
the clitoris has only been very recently revealed.

According to Freud, childhood and puberty are fraught with sexual
pitfalls and one false step along the way can lead to any number of
problems in later life.

* The object choice begins with the child's early relationships with
  parents and carers. It is only later diverted away to other people by
  incest taboos.

* The child can get stuck at any stage in the sexual development
  process. This is called **fixation**.

* Repression of sexual urges may lead to psychoneurotic illness, such
  as perversion.

* Very often the libido finds an outlet in another, non-sexual field.
  This is called sublimation (see Chapter 5).

Freud suggests that neurotic people may have a greater tendency to be
affected by early sexual experiences, and a greater tendency to be become
fixated. He saw one of the main causes of fixation to be the early seduction of the child by another child or an adult. He suggested that sexual

deviations could arise through a combination of several causes such as:

* a compliant constitution, and/or precocity;

* increased susceptibility to early sexual experiences;

* chance stimulation of the sexual instinct by external influences, a foot fetish brought about by an early encounter with velvet slippers.

***

* * * *SUMMARY* * * *

● Freud's views on sexuality, particularly that of infants, caused great uproar in his contemporaties.

● He said that the sexual instinct was a lot more complicated than people had previously maintained.

● Sexual impulses are present from birth, but are soon overcome by a progressive process of repression.

● The sexuality of neurotics and deviants has usually remained in, or been brought back to, an infantile state.

● Childhood and puberty are fraught with sexual pitfalls and development can go wrong or get stuck at any stage.

Going Back to Childhood

Freud gradually developed his ideas about childhood sexuality in order to try and explain how people developed into social beings. He eventually divided psychosexual development into several definite stages. Each stage followed on from the one before in a biologically determined manner and the way a person coped with each stage influenced their adult personality. Freud did not explain these all at once in a neat and logical order, but added to his theories over a period of many years. The ideas are therefore scattered in different parts of his writing.

The development of the personality is a progress through various stages. Each stage is concerned with ways in which children experience sexual pleasure at that particular phase of development. Sexuality is a dominant theme in Freud's work and he was concerned with the ways in which the libido can become blocked or re-directed.

THE ORAL STAGE

This is the first stage of development and lasts from birth to about one year. The infant indulges in sucking various parts of the body, especially the thumb, an activity that follows on from sucking the mother's breast. The sucking is rhythmic, and often involves rubbing movements as well. Freud says that these later lead on to masturbation. The activity is very absorbing and comforting and often sends the infant off to sleep.

Sucking is obviously by far the most important activity at this stage in the baby's life, and so the mother becomes the first love object. The baby feels love or hate accordingly, as the breast is offered or withdrawn. The source of love is also the food source, and it gradually becomes a source of sexual pleasure. Freud broadened the concept of sexual pleasure, allowing it also to encompass sensual pleasure.

Withdrawal of the breast is seen as withdrawal of love, and fixation at this stage is called 'oral fixation'. Freud says that this fixation sometimes occurs when babies have not been breast-fed. It manifests later in different ways, for example:

* thumb-sucking in older children;

* chewing gum, pens, pencils, finger nails etc;

* smoking, over-eating or over-drinking;

* feeling a constant need to be loved.

This seems to cover the vast majority of the adult population, so presumably we are not very good at getting past this first stage!

THE ANAL STAGE

This lasts from about the age of one to three years, and coincides with the 'potty training' phase, when the child learns to control the bladder and bowels. The child feels very proud when he or she produces stools and often sees them as part of him or herself. However, the adults who care for the child may express disgust, especially if the child produces offerings at an inappropriate time or place. The child has to learn when the activity is socially acceptable and when it is not.

The child soon finds that it can gain power over the adult by withholding stools, or by producing them at the wrong time. According to Freud, producing or withholding stools is all very pleasurable. When potty training begins, the baby often deliberately hangs onto its stools because it wants to enjoy the erotic pleasure of producing the stool in private! Producing a huge stool also apparently causes a wonderful stimulation of the mucous membrane of the anus. (A more acceptable argument today is that stool retention happens because the baby is constipated and producing huge compacted stools hurts.)

The anal phase is where social conditioning really begins to come into play. The child is praised for being 'clean' and getting things 'right'. On the other hand, repressive guilt and disgust begin to appear when the child gets it 'wrong'. Fixation at this stage can take more than one form.

* **Anal expulsiveness** follows on from producing stools inappropriately.

Adults stuck at this stage are often scruffy, disordered and anti-social.

* **Anal retentiveness** follows on from the withholding of stools. The adult stuck at this stage is compulsively neat and tidy, orderly and conformist.

Parental disapproval at this stage can also lead to a later neurotic obsession with dirt and cleaning.

THE PHALLIC STAGE

Passing on the anal fixation.

This stage lasts from about three to five years. The genitals now become the erogenous zone and the child starts to masturbate. The infant genital zone is stimulated frequently by washing, rubbing dry, peeing and so on. The child soon learns to stimulate the area itself, by rubbing with the hand or by pressing the thighs together. Freud's views on this stage reveal a misogynist attitude – the phallus is seen as all-important, and in fact he seems to regard it as the *only* sexual organ. This is the stage where sexual differences are often discovered by children, giving rise to castration complex in boys and penis envy in girls (see Chapter 6). Girls see themselves as already castrated and never really recover from the shock of the revelation about penises.

Freud claimed that all children believe at this stage that they can either give their mother a baby, or else produce one themselves by giving birth anally. This curious theory perhaps serves to underline the dangers of trying to evolve theories about normal child development from working with neurotic adults! This is also the stage when the **Oedipus complex** emerges.

KEYWORDS

Complex: a related group of ideas that are usually repressed and cause emotional problems and conflicts.

Oedipus complex: desire of the child to possess sexually the parent of the opposite sex, while excluding the parent of the same sex.

THE OEDIPUS COMPLEX

Freud formed his ideas about the Oedipus complex during the period of his own self-analysis (see Chapter 3). In a letter to Fliess at this time he describes discovering that as a small boy he had been in love with his mother and jealous of his father. The Oedipus complex is named after a character in an ancient Greek story. Oedipus was the son of King Laius and Queen Jocasta of Thebes. It was prophesied that Oedipus would murder his father and marry his mother, and so in fear his father had him left exposed to die on the mountain soon after his birth. However, the baby was rescued by shepherds and brought up by a foreign king and queen.

Eventually Oedipus met his father by chance on the road to Thebes, and murdered him in a fit of rage. He then went to Thebes and rid the city of a tiresome Sphinx, who had been eating anybody who was unable to answer her riddle correctly. Oedipus answered the riddle and was rewarded by being made king, and so ended up unknowingly marrying his mother, Jocasta. Eventually Oedipus found out what he had done, and blinded himself as a punishment.

In putting forward his theories on the Oedipus complex, Freud argued the following.

* All little boys of about four or five fall in love with their mothers.

* The boy expresses his desire in various ways, such as by announcing that he is going to marry her, or by insisting on climbing into bed with her all the time.

* He becomes curious about her naked body.

* The boy wants total possession of the mother and becomes jealous of his father and wants to kill him to get him out of the way.

* Because the father is obviously so big and powerful, the boy is afraid that he will be punished by his father castrating him. This fear eventually makes him abandon his mother as a sexual object.

The picture Freud paints for girls is even more bizarre and he is typically much less clear about his views.

* The little girl is also involved with lusting after the mother initially, but then comes the awful revelation that she has no penis.

* The little girl believes she has lost hers and (for some obscure reason) blames her mother for this.

* The little girl cannot fear castration because she sees herself as already castrated. For her the corresponding fear is a fear of loss of love.

* She then turns to the father as a sex object, hoping that he will impregnate her. The resulting baby would partly make up for the lost penis.

* The conflict is gradually resolved as she turns her attention away from her father towards other men.

Freud saw the Oedipal conflict as being basic to psychosexual development. Failure to resolve the incestuous conflict would result in neurosis later in life.

OEDIPUSS   PUSS PUSS...

The author's Oedipus complex develops new complications following a visit to her grandparents.

To us today the theory can seem contrived, but this is partly because it has been overstated by Freud. He seems to make the mistake of generalizing on the basis of his own childhood experiences. However, if we look at the theory again we can see some elements of truth in it.

* Small boys do sometimes seem to fall in love with their mothers, and may consequently get very jealous of the father.

* The same is true with small girls and their fathers.

* The blinding of Oedipus is symbolic of the shock, self-disgust and self-punishment that may arise when dark inner wishes are revealed. Many people do feel guilty about their own natural sexual urges.

* Men and boys sometimes do fear damage to the penis – it is rather vulnerable after all. In the past, little boys were actually threatened with having their penis cut off if they masturbated, which would obviously lead to considerable anxiety.

✳ In Freud's day, girls were seen as being very inferior and making a baby was probably one of the few important things they could do.

THE LATENCY STAGE
According to Freud the feelings from the Oedipal stage are eventually suppressed and the sexual drive becomes dormant until puberty. In fact subsequent research has shown that this is not really the case and that, on the contrary, sexual curiosity, sexual play and masturbation all gradually increase. However, in Freud's time such activity would have been concealed from adults.

THE GENITAL STAGE
The final stage in development is the genital stage, which takes place from puberty onwards. There is now a renewal of sexual interest and a new object is found for the sex drive. This is seen as the final stage, the completion of development, which seems rather odd considering the angst and confusion most of us go through in our teens and early adulthood! The Oedipus complex is now resolved and the natural aim of the sex drive becomes sexual intercourse with an opposite-sex adult.

Freud insisted that **psychosexual** development was central to all social and emotional development. His theories about the way the child's sexuality developed provided a model of the way the whole personality developed. Freud did not say that the whole mind was only

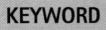

KEYWORD

Psychosexual: relating to the mental aspects of sex, such as sexual fantasy.

concerned with sex – otherwise there would be no conflicts. Much of the opposition to his theories has arisen because of the way he defined 'sexual'. For him the concept had a much broader meaning than just sex itself. Nevertheless, most people now feel that his emphasis on the sexual was exaggerated.

✳ ✳ ✳ ✳ *SUMMARY* ✳ ✳ ✳ ✳

- Freud's definition of what was sexual was broad.

- His theories about how children developed sexually became a model for social and psychological development in general.

- Normal sexual development was seen as going through defined stages that were the same in all children.

- People could get stuck at any stage – this was called 'fixation'.

- Freud developed a ground-breaking theory called the Oedipus complex to explain the basis of psychosexual development.

Seeking an Adult Identity

Freud gradually developed his theories about the ways in which the adult personality is formed and structured. For a long time he struggled with the problem of how neuroses arose. He knew that unacceptable or frightening ideas were repressed and banished to the unconscious – but where did this repression come from?

In 1923 Freud proposed a new **dynamic model** of the mind. This involved three main parts: the id, ego and **super-ego**. These are not parts of the brain, but represent different aspects of the way we think. They attempt to explain the apparent battle that goes on between different levels of consciousness.

THE ID

From the Latin word for 'it', the id is the primitive unconscious part of the mind that we are born with. It is a dark, inaccessible area, seething with instinctive urges and its only reality is its own selfish needs. It is the source of the motive force behind the pleasure principle. As a child develops through the various oral, anal and phallic stages, it begins to realize that the world 'out there' is real too. This new awareness is closely linked to sexual development. Gradually the child begins to realize that it cannot always instantly have what it wants, and begins to suppress the id urges in order to fit in with society.

Adults who are selfish or impulsive may be unable or unwilling to suppress the id. The desires of the id are commonly expressed in dreams.

THE EGO

From the Latin word for 'I', the ego is the part of the mind which reacts to external reality and which a person thinks of as the 'self'. The ego is where consciousness comes from, although not all of its functions are carried out consciously.

* The ego tells us what is 'real'. It is a 'synthesiser' or a 'maker of sense'.

* It is practical and rational, and is involved in decision-making.

* Anxiety arises from the ego. This is seen as a mechanism for warning us that there is a weakness somewhere in the ego's defences.

* A whole system of unconscious **defence mechanisms** protects the ego.

* The ego is seen as being rather weak in comparison with the id, but it is better organized and more logical, so that it usually maintains a tenuous upper hand.

Freud explains, somewhat confusingly, that the ego is part of the id, which develops in order to cope with threats from the outside world. He compares the ego and the id with a rider and his horse. The horse supplies the motor energy, but the rider decides where to go. The ego constantly has to devise plans to satisfy the id in a controlled way. For example, a child is hungry but knows that it will have to wait until teatime until it gets a slice of cake.

THE SUPER-EGO

A very small child is amoral and has little sense of inhibition. Any controls over its behaviour are provided by the parents and carers who look after it. In normal development this state of affairs slowly changes. The super-ego develops as the Oedipus complex begins to be resolved. As the repression of Oedipal urges commences, the child feels a mixture of love, fear and hostility towards the parents. Gradually a sort of inner parent evolves and the child has feelings of guilt, of being 'watched' and controlled. This is the super-ego.

* The super-ego gives us our sense of right and wrong, pride and guilt.

* It often gets us to act in ways that are acceptable to the society, rather

than to us as individuals. For example, it might make a person feel guilty for having extra-marital sex. The super-ego incorporates the teachings of the past and of tradition.

* It monitors behaviour, decides what is acceptable and controls taboo.

* It is bossy, always demanding perfection of the ego.

The way the super-ego works is in a sense opposite to that of the id. The id wants to satisfy the needs of the individual, regardless of what society wants. Like the ego, large parts of the super-ego can operate in unconscious ways. Freud acknowledges that the distinctions between id, ego and super-ego are not easy to grasp and that the three are not always sharply separated. If an adult has a reasonably mature, mentally healthy personality, the id, ego and super-ego will be acting in a balanced way.

ANXIETY

Conflicts between the different aspects of the personality result in anxiety and stress. Freud said that anxiety acts as an alarm signal that something is wrong. He identified three types of anxiety.

* **Realistic anxiety**: this arises from real events in the external world, perceived by the ego.

* **Neurotic anxiety**: this arises from the id, and often seems enigmatic and unfocused. It is not necessarily connected with external events in the real world.

* **Moral anxiety**: this arises from the super-ego – it is the voice of the conscience, telling us when something is 'improper'.

Anxiety from all three sources feels similar, and in fact anxiety can arise from a mixture of different sources at the same time. Anxiety is closely associated with feelings of guilt. It can also present itself in the form of phobias and hysteria. Hysterical anxiety can come as a very severe attack, which does not necessarily have an obvious source in the external world.

Freud says that the most common cause of anxiety is sexual frustration.

This begins in infancy, when the mother is not present, or the infant sees an unfamiliar face. (Remember that Freud sees the mother as the sex object at this stage – see Chapter 7.) A particular source of anxiety is attached to each developmental stage. For example, at the phallic stage it is the fear of castration that causes anxiety and at the latency stage it is a developing fear of the super-ego. As the ego gets stronger and more clearly defined the anxieties weaken, but traces of them usually remain. Neurotics remain infantile in their attitude to danger and consequently suffer a great deal from anxiety.

DEFENCE MECHANISMS

Defence mechanisms arise in order to protect the ego from too much anxiety. Without them the anxiety can become a threat to mental health. Defence mechanisms are used unconsciously, and within reason they are healthy. However, they can easily become too forceful and damaging, requiring much mental effort to sustain them, and masking issues that really need to be addressed. They become a strategy for hiding from anxiety.

Repression

This is one of the most common defence mechanisms and forms the basis for many of Freud's theories. Undesirable information is stored away in the unconscious, so repression is really a form of forgetting. We may repress something so that we do not have to deal with painful feelings and memories. People can lose whole blocks of time in this way after a traumatic event, and conscious efforts to recall events have no effect. This can apply to both emotional traumas and traumas caused by external events, such as war.

Denial

Denial is closely related to repression, but this time the person refuses to accept the reality of a situation. This is sometimes acceptable as a short-term defence, but become dangerous if the situation is never properly dealt with. For example, a person may find a suspicious lump somewhere on their body and, fearing it might be cancer may forget all about it rather than go to the doctor.

Displacement

This is another common defence mechanism that arises as a result of repression. Because a person cannot release a basic feeling such as anger, it builds up and is then directed towards another person, animal or object that has nothing to do with the original situation. For example, if a person has a bad day at work, rather than confront the boss they may come home and vent their frustration on the family.

Displacement can also appear passively, where a person constantly complains and demands attention. The mystifying inscrutable silence, conveying the unspoken message that one has 'done something' can be another of its unpleasant passive variations.

Projection

This is almost a combination of both denial and displacement. It is once again a result of repression, whereby a person is unable to recognize the reality of his or her own behaviour. The result is that taboo urges or faults are projected outwards onto another person. For example, the bossiest member of the household covers up by accusing one of the others of being bossy.

Fantasy

Most people indulge in a certain amount of fantasy and daydreaming in order to make life more bearable. This can be positive – for example, dreaming of that holiday in Spain might motivate you to work a little harder. It is only harmful when a person can no longer separate fantasy from reality. When this happens a person may spend so much psychic energy on fantasy that they do not address things that are blocking progress in real life.

Rationalization

Projection.

Here a person finds an excuse for their behaviour that is more acceptable to the ego than the real reason. For example, the driver of a car might say: 'I took the wrong turning there because I was so busy trying to avoid that wretched cyclist who was all over the road.' This conveniently covers up the fact that actually they were not paying attention to where they were going in the first place.

Regression

Regression is another defence mechanism that we have already met. Here the person reverts back to an earlier behaviour or developmental stage that feels safe or comforting. We all tend to do it if we feel ill or upset. It is very common in children who want more attention, perhaps because of a new baby, or because their parents are getting divorced. Adults sometimes go into a severe regression after a ghastly trauma, and may even curl up into a foetal position.

Reaction formation

Sometimes a person feels an impulse and covers it up by displaying its exact opposite, for example, by being pleasant and polite to somebody they actually want to be rude to. Reaction formation as a form of defence is quite common in teenagers, and is often shown by an individual being hostile to somebody they are really attracted to. The problem arises when the latent urge remains dormant and unresolved, and so may build up into a powerfully negative force.

> **KEYWORD**
>
> Reaction formation: covering up an impulse by displaying the opposite behaviour.

TRANSFERENCE

Any of the defence mechanisms can actually be helpful and they all appear in the behaviour of normal, healthy people. Problems only arise when they are overdone and the person becomes blind to their true feelings and motives. The job of the psychoanalyst is to help people to unravel these. This can be a very painful process, but it is one that helps us towards a more balanced personality.

During the course of psychoanalytic treatment, it is normal for some transference to take place – in fact it is part of the healing process. The patient may direct feelings of love or hostility towards the analyst. This is helpful because it re-creates the original problem in miniature. Freud called this a 'transference neurosis'. The advantage is that unconscious feelings are now out in the open and can be examined and hopefully dealt with properly.

NARCISSISM

Freud found some patients who did not respond to psychoanalytic therapy at all. He used the myth of Narcissus to explain this. Narcissus was a beautiful youth in ancient Greece who fell in love with his own reflection in a pool. He pined away and eventually died and was turned into a flower because he could never fully possess himself. Freud saw this story as a good way of illustrating the idea of an ego that has become totally self-absorbed and can no longer relate to the outside world. Such cases of psychosis are not treatable by psychoanalysis, because the normal transference does not occur.

Narcissism is normal in infancy, when the infantile ego expects the outside world to be just the same as itself. It is also normal for some degree of self-love to appear within any adult relationship

MOURNING AND MELANCHOLIA

Freud produced work under this title in 1915, which can be found in *The Standard Edition of the Complete Works of Sigmund Freud* (see Further Reading). We would now call melancholia severe depression. This often occurs after a bereavement or divorce and shows itself in many ways.

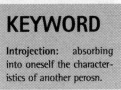

KEYWORD

Introjection: absorbing into oneself the characteristics of another perosn.

* The person blames themself for what has happened and becomes self-destructive, even suicidal.

* The person becomes withdrawn from the world, as in Narcissism, but this time the self is seen as being bad, unworthy, dirty, etc.

* Severe mourning can conceal repressed hatred for the lost person. The lost person becomes identified with the patient's own ego, so that hate becomes self-hate and guilt. This is called **introjection**.

* The person may regress to an infantile state, where biting, sucking and excreting are dominant. They will be absorbed with images of excreta and filth. They are unable to express their mixed feelings of love and hate directly.

INSTINCTS

It is not always clear what Freud means when he talks about 'instincts'. In fact, he says that they are a very vague concept, 'magnificent in their indefiniteness'. He complains that people are forever inventing new instincts in order to explain different aspects of behaviour, such as love, hunger and aggression. Freud turned to biology for help, trying as always to be scientific in his approach. This was not easy, because science concerns itself with external, observable reality, whereas Freud was grappling with the workings of the mind.

According to Freud, current biological thinking grouped instincts into two types, according to the aim of the behaviour involved. The first type was aimed at self-preservation, the second at preservation of the species. Freud carried this idea over into psychoanalysis and therefore classified instincts in two ways.

* **Ego instincts**: concerned with the needs of the individual.

* **Sexual instincts**: concerned with preserving the species.

Freud tried to clarify what he meant by an instinct by contrasting it with a stimulus. A stimulus, he said, arises from things going on outside the body. Instincts arise from within, and cannot be avoided by running away. The instinct is identified by its:

* **source**: excitation within the body;

* **aim**: removal of that excitation;

* **object**: usually external.

EROS AND THANATOS

For a long time Freud was puzzled by the tendency for patients to go on repeating and reliving unpleasant experiences. He called this **repetition compulsion**. He found that it happens after a sudden and unexpected shock. Freud decided that the experience was repeated so that the normal anxiety that prepares us for danger could be built up and dealt with in

KEYWORDS

Reptition compulsion: inner drive that causes an individual to repeat actions.

Thanatos: destructive behaviour either to the self or to others.

retrospect. However, the repetition compulsion can sometimes totally take over. This phenomenon eventually led Freud to suggest that another instinct was at work – **Thanatos,** or the death instinct. The word *thanatos* is taken from the Greek word meaning 'death'.

When Thanatos is directed towards the self it produces self-destructive behaviour, such as addictions in which the individual is 'dicing with death'. Turned outwards it results in aggressive behaviour. The opposite of Thanatos is **Eros**, the life instinct (from Eros, the Greek god of love). It is concerned with survival of the species and is responsible for sexual and reproductive behaviour.

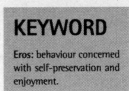

KEYWORD

Eros: behaviour concerned with self-preservation and enjoyment.

Freud's argument for the existence of Thanatos can be summarized as follows.

* All behaviour is aimed at reducing tension and achieving a previously existing state of stability.

* Since we were all originally made from inert matter, then perhaps we are really trying all the time to return to this state.

* So the aim of all life is death, a state where there are no tensions at all.

This seems like a very negative way of looking at things, but this perhaps arose partly because Freud's own life became very difficult and full of pain. He lived through the horrors of World War I and then suffered the death of a daughter in 1920 and a grandson in 1923. His first operation for oral cancer came in 1923 – the first of 33 such operations, that must have left him in constant pain and discomfort for the rest of his life. It is to his credit that he never gave up, but kept on thinking and working until the end.

＊＊＊＊SUMMARY＊＊＊＊

● Freud established a useful new model of the ways in which we develop into adult human beings.

● He provided a map of the different levels of thinking and behaviour, which he called id, ego and super-ego.

● Instinctive drives are held in check by a complex system of defence mechanisms. These appear in normal people as well as neurotics.

● Problems in the defence system can eventually lead to neurosis or even psychosis.

● Freud identified two opposing instincts that he called Eros and Thanatos, the life instinct and the death instinct.

The Psychoanalytic Movement

9

EARLY BEGINNINGS

In 1902 Freud was appointed as a professor at the University of Vienna. This was mainly because of his work in the field of neurology. People in the medical and academic world were still reacting with hostility and suspicion to his controversial ideas about psychoanalysis. Freud carried on with these ideas more or less alone, but gradually a small band of followers began to gather around him. He set up a small group of like-minded people called the Wednesday Psychological Society, and they would meet in his waiting room. This small group included Wilhelm Stekel (Austrian writer and psychotherapist) and Alfred Adler (Austrian Jew, an opthalmologist and psychiatrist). Each week one of the members would give a talk about new ideas, followed by refreshments and then a discussion.

The group soon expanded and by 1906 there were 17 members. Eventually the group evolved into the Vienna Psychoanalytic Society. Otto Rank (Austrian, non-medical analyst. First and most valued pupil of Freud) was appointed as secretary and he kept minutes of the meetings and accounts. By 1907 the group was getting more cosmopolitan – a Russian called Max Eitingon joined them, followed by some Swiss recruits from the Burghölzli Mental Hospital in Zurich. These were Ludwig Binswanger, Carl Jung and Karl Abraham. Freud and Jung got on especially well and a kind of father–son relationship developed between them, Freud being nearly twenty years older than Jung. Freud was particularly pleased that Jung was a Gentile, because this rescued the psychoanalytic movement from accusations that it was an all-Jewish organization.

Over the next year the Hungarian doctor Sándor Ferenczi, joined the group, and then Ernest Jones, a young Welsh neurologist, and Abraham Brill from America. Eitingon and Abraham went on to establish psychoanalysis in Berlin, and Ferenczi in Budapest. Jones and Brill were the first to introduce psychoanalytic thinking into the English language. The first International Congress of Freudian Psychology took place in Salzburg in 1908.

By 1909 Freud was well known internationally and he accompanied Jung and Ferenczi to America to lecture. The first *International Journal of Psychoanalysis* was published the same year, and Freud was awarded an honorary degree from Clark University, Massachusetts. The next year the International Psychoanalytic Association was formed. International progress was fairly slow until the end of the World War I. In 1920 the Institute of Psychoanalysis was opened in Berlin, followed by further openings in London, Vienna and Budapest. Courses were held for students and free treatment offered to people who could not afford the fees. Institutes were opened in America in New York (1931) and Chicago (1932).

RIFTS IN THE PSYCHOANALYTIC MOVEMENT

Right from the start there tended to be arguments and disagreements within the psychoanalytic movement. People were keen to develop their own theories and some accused others of inventing case histories to fit their theories. Arguments arose about the way the society was organized, and about psychoanalytic methods and concepts such as the unconscious. To make matters worse, the group was constantly under outside attack from the scientific establishment and the press.

Alfred Adler

Adler was a Viennese Jew, and one of the first members of the Wednesday group. He did not agree with the idea of repressed sexual impulses being the cause of neurosis. He maintained that the urges that caused all the trouble were aggressive ones, not sexual. Adler believed that a person's biological make-up was the most important thing. If a person had a particular handicap, then they would work all the harder in order to overcome feelings of inferiority.

Adler had been President of the Vienna Society, but he resigned in 1911. He was followed in 1912 by Stekel, who refused to believe in the overwhelming importance of the unconscious. Meanwhile an underground group, initiated by Ernest Jones, rallied round to support Freud. Despite the influence of this inner circle, the group gradually lost further members.

Otto Rank
Rank had been a protégé of Freud, who had encouraged and supported his education. For a long time he was loyal to Freud, but eventually he was thrown out of the group. His main complaint was that he felt the period of analysis was too long and he suggested that it should be shortened. He also saw childhood traumas, especially the Oedipus complex, as being less important than Freud suggested. For him it was the trauma of birth itself that mattered.

Carl Jung
Jung was Freud's favourite for some years. Freud treated him like a son and wanted him to be his successor. In 1910 he was appointed as the President of the newly formed International Psychoanalytic Society. However, there had already been suggestions of problems in his relationship with Freud before then.

The year before, while they were waiting to board ship to go to America, tension was in the air. Freud had found out that Jung had been having an illicit affair with one of his patients. Jung retaliated by being hostile towards Freud. He irritated him by going on and on about mummified peat bog men that were being dug up in north Germany. Freud got very het up and eventually fainted. Later he said that this was because Jung had a death wish against him.

Worse was to come as Jung began to develop new theories of his own. He had had reservations from the beginning, feeling that Freud tended to put him on a pedestal. His own feelings were very intense too – he said that it was almost as if he had a teenage crush on Freud. Freud had also recognized that this intensity of feeling might ultimately end in some sort of teenage rebellion.

In 1912 Jung gave a series of lectures and seminars at Fordham University in New York. It was at this point that he really broke away from Freud, criticizing the basic theories of psychoanalysis by saying that:

* the Oedipus complex was not of central importance, although he acknowledged its existence and coined the term 'Electra complex' for its equivalent in women;

* libido should not be regarded as merely sexual but as a universal life force;

* Freud's ideas about infant sexuality were wrong – Jung proposed that sexuality developed more gradually;

* pleasure could come from all sorts of non-sexual sources. For example, a baby gains pleasure from sucking because it is fulfilling a nutritional need;

* adult neuroses were rooted in current problems that sometimes resurrected old conflicts. These were not necessarily infantile conflicts, nor were they always sexual.

Not long after this attack on the core concepts of psychoanalysis, Freud talked to Jung at length at a conference in Munich in 1912 and felt that he had won him back into the fold. Freud then proceeded to faint again at lunch, and Jung had to carry him through into another room. Clearly Freud was deeply upset about the whole affair.

The next year Jung lectured in London and talked once again about wanting to move psychoanalysis away from its narrow emphasis on sex. He coined the phrase 'analytical psychology' to describe the ideas that he was evolving. After this, letters between Freud and Jung became increasingly bitter. Jung accused Freud of behaving like a controlling father, intolerant towards new ideas. Sadly, in 1913 their friendship ceased altogether and the two men became openly hostile to one another. Before long Jung resigned his presidency of the International Psychoanalytical Society.

Wilhelm Reich

Reich was another member of the orthodox psychoanalytical movement who broke away much later, in 1933. He was interested in the way individuals interacted with society and believed that a person's character was formed in this way. For him the sexual revolution was connected with the social revolution. He worked with the communist party, thus combining psychoanalysis with politics.

Most of the people who broke away from Freud did so because they felt that he laid too much emphasis on sex. Psychoanalysis was very difficult to understand and people were constantly coming up with new variations of their own. Freud tended to present a rather authoritarian figure, always trying to keep control and resenting the intrusion of new ideas from others. It is amusing to think of him as a sort of struggling super-ego of the psychoanalytic movement, desperately trying to control all the other egos!

SOME FAMOUS FOLLOWERS OF FREUD

Anna was Freud's youngest daughter and she nursed him through his last illness. She was a pupil of his and eventually became a psychoanalyst in her own right and an important member of the International Psychoanalytical Association. She concentrated mainly on the ego and the various ways in which it defended itself, because she believed that there had previously been too much emphasis on the id. She was very much a supporter of her father's original ideas, but she developed and extended them. Anna believed that it was very important to look at defence mechanisms because they help us to understand what the problems are that the ego is grappling with. She identified the main dangers to the ego as:

* instinctual urges from the id;

* nagging from the super-ego;

* external dangers;

* conflict within the ego, caused by opposing tendencies, such as activity and passivity.

Anna fled from the Nazis before World War II and eventually co-founded the Hampstead Child Therapy Clinic in London. Anna's ideas are important mainly because she derived them from direct observation of young children, rather than by talking to adults about their childhood. She was a pioneer in working with psychologically disturbed children.

Melanie Klein

Melanie Klein was born in Vienna and underwent analysis with Sándor Ferenczi, before working in his children's clinic. She moved to London in 1926 and became a British citizen. Like Anna Freud, her main contribution came from her work with children, although she also worked with disturbed adults. Melanie Klein believed that emotions were present in children from a very young age. She observed children's emotions by watching them at play, even before they could express themselves verbally. This new way of working with children led to her being able to analyse them at a much earlier age than had previously been thought possible, even as young as two years old.

Melanie Klein believed that the forerunner of the super-ego began to form during the first two years of life. For her the aggressive drive was the important one, rather than the sexual drive. Her arguments caused disagreements in mainstream psychoanalysis with some people, such as Anna Freud. Others, especially in England, saw her as Freud's successor. She was one of the leading lights in the Object Relations School. This school of thought disagreed with Freud's stages of development. It said that right from birth the mental life of a child is orientated towards an object. The object can be anything in the external world – a person or a thing. The child constructs its inner world from ideas about these external objects. Conflicts arise as a result of the way in which this 'internalization' process progresses.

Karen Horney

Karen Horney was an analyst in Berlin during the 1920s and 1930s and later joined the staff at the New York Psychoanalytical Institute. She was particularly interested in social factors in psychological development and eventually her ideas evolved away from the mainstream. Many people in the psychoanalytical movement have taken a rather closed shop attitude, saying that anyone who is not an analyst will never be able to fully understand psychoanalytical theory. Like Adler, Karen Horney wrote for the general reader and her ideas became very popular in America.

Karen Horney maintained that social influences are much more important than underlying fixed biological patterns in developing neuroses. She said that the latter idea was too deterministic and out of date. She argued against the idea of an Oedipus complex, saying that there was no such thing as a universal child psychology.

Karen Horney was also interested in women's psychology. She said that women's feelings of inferiority were caused by oppression from society, rather than by a biologically determined castration complex.

Erich Fromm

Fromm was born in Germany and trained as a social psychologist and psychoanalyst. Later he worked with Karen Horney and H. S. Sullivan. He was interested in the individual's relationship with society. He said that different cultures produce different psychological types. The work of anthropologists since has tended to back up his ideas. The Oedipus complex has indeed turned out not to be universal – there are big differences in child-rearing habits, family structure, social rules and so on.

Fromm's ideas differed from those of Freud in two fundamental ways.

* A person's main challenge comes from the way he or she relates to others in society and not from the struggle with instinctual urges.

* Relationships between mankind and society are constantly changing. Freud had taken the view that the relationship was static – mankind was basically evil and society's job was to tame him.

H.S. Sullivan

Sullivan was another psychiatrist influenced by Freud who believed that the personality was influenced by society. This view is called the 'culturalist view'. Sullivan said that a person felt happy and 'good' if his behaviour fitted in with societal norms. If the reverse was true then the person felt 'bad' and insecure.

＊＊＊＊SUMMARY＊＊＊＊

• The psychoanalytical movement grew slowly from humble beginnings in Vienna to become a movement of international importance.

• Right from the start there were arguments and disagreements within the group. Many people broke away, mainly because they disagreed with Freud's emphasis on the importance of the sexual.

• Many influential psychologists and psychiatrists have been inspired by Freud and have developed his ideas further.

Freud and Society

10

CIVILIZATION

Freud saw civilization as representing the ways in which human life has raised itself above its animal origins. Civilization demands great sacrifices from the individual, because instinctual urges have to be suppressed all the time in order to conform. The purpose of human life is the pursuit of happiness, dominated by the pleasure principle. By happiness, Freud means satisfaction of libidinous needs that often become dammed up. The ego has to find ways of controlling such urges, sublimating them so that society will approve of behaviour. Living in society is therefore difficult and it is hard for people to be happy.

The features of civilized living are seen by Freud as being beauty, order and cleanliness. Justice is the first requirement in maintaining these – the law must not be broken in favour of the individual. The two main reasons for living together in societies are:

* the need to get together in order to share the workload;

* security within relationships, e.g. man and woman, woman and child.

In order to gain these advantages people must curb sexual and aggressive urges. This is why it is difficult to live in a society and be happy. Consequently, aggressive urges may be turned inwards towards the self, causing a sense of guilt and a need for punishment. This is the essence of the Oedipal complex, whereby the instinctual urge is repressed for fear of action by external authority and gradually the internal sense of authority, the super-ego, takes over. Freud says that the sense of guilt is the most important problem in the development of civilization. Any thwarted instinctual urge heightens the sense of guilt and increases the problem of people trying to live happily together.

The conflicting needs of society and the individual leads to a constant battle between ego and altruism. The essence of this battle is 'do I answer my own needs, or do I try to fit in with other people?' Freud suggests that this battle is what causes neurosis and that it is possible that entire civilizations can develop a sort of mass neurosis and a communal super-ego. An obvious example would be the dictator leading the mass of followers. Freud's view of human nature became increasingly disillusioned and he felt that people constantly over-valued power, status and wealth. These ideas certainly have a prophetic ring to them in the modern world.

THOUGHTS ABOUT WAR

During World War I, Freud at first supported the Austro-German Alliance for which members of his family fought. However, he was a pacifist at heart and became very disillusioned with war.

He expressed his bewilderment as the nations of the civilized world slaughtered one another and destroyed so much that science, technology and art had strived to achieve. Freud recognized the gap between what passes as acceptable behaviour for a state and what is expected of the individual. He also saw that the state demanded complete obedience from its people, and yet treated them like children by its censorship of the truth. His sense of disillusionment increased as he observed:

* the low morality shown in the behaviour of states;
* the brutality that emerged in the behaviour of individuals, who used war as an excuse to unleash aggression.

Freud said that these two observations proved that deep down human nature consists of instinctual impulses, therefore we can never totally eradicate evil. A person can be 'good' in one set of circumstances and 'bad' in another. People conform and obey because they need both love and fear punishment.

Freud is not really trying to say that it is impossible for humans to behave in a civilized fashion. He actually says that people have over-estimated their own capabilities – we are not as highly evolved as we had thought we were. If we were less demanding of ourselves, this would lead to less disillusionment and the ability to be more open and honest.

The war made Freud think about people's attitudes towards death. He said that before the war people had tended to pretend that death did not exist. War forced them to believe in it and took them back to a primeval state when death was part of life's daily struggle, and man had no scruples about killing. It was Freud's work with victims of war trauma and shell shock that led him to develop his ideas about repetition compulsion (whereby the sufferer repeats often trivial actions) and Thanatos, the death instinct (see Chapter 8).

Freud lived to see the start of the World War II as well. Hitler had come to power in Germany in 1933 and there was a public burning of Freud's books in Berlin. Freud saw this as progress, saying that in the Middle Ages they would have burned him too. How wrong he was – fortunately Freud was spared the horror of the holocaust, although several members of his family were victims. One wonders what he would have thought and felt about it. His fellowship with Jews mattered to him and he had belonged to a Jewish club in Vienna, even though he did not follow the Jewish religion.

Another Jew to flee from Nazism was Albert Einstein and a letter from him in 1932 persuaded Freud to write again about war. Freud replied that war was more a problem for statesmen to worry about, but he tried to arrive at some psychological insights.

* Usually conflicts of interest among humans are settled by the use of violence.

* Several weak people can combine to overcome one strong one.

* A community is held together by emotional ties.

* Problems arise within a community when suppressed members begin to want more power.

* The instincts of love and hate are both essential – you cannot have one without the other.

Freud concluded that war could only be prevented if a central authority was set up which had the right to settle all conflicts of interest. To this end he suggested in his letter to Einstein educating a special elite, with independent open minds, who would 'give direction to the dependent masses'. (This sounds curiously similar to what the Nazis had in mind.) In the final paragraph of the letter, Freud speaks of himself and, by implication, Einstein, as pacifists. But he adds 'there is no telling' how long it will be until the rest of mankind follows suit.

ART AND LITERATURE

Freud's work on the unconscious and the use of free association techniques have had an enormous effect upon both art and literature. Artists began to experiment a lot more with imagery from dreams, visions and the unconscious. This led to movements such as **surrealism**. The idea

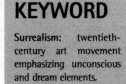

KEYWORD

Surrealism: twentieth-century art movement emphasizing unconscious and dream elements.

was not actually new – as long ago as the fifteenth century, Hieronymus Bosch became famous for his grotesque and fantastic imagery – but Freud's ideas led to a great fresh upsurge in interest.

Biographers began to examine intimate sexual details and childhood experiences of their subjects, and novelists began to use new techniques such as the 'stream of consciousness'. This method, used for example by Virginia Woolf (1882–1941), gives the reader a detailed account of all that the character is thinking from moment to moment. It has obvious connections with the free association technique.

Freud believed that all art and literature was the result of the sublimation of libidinous urges. Daydreams and fantasies were ways of evading the tedious grip of the reality principle. Artists and writers actually allowed themselves to live in their fantasy world, so effectively evading the reality principle and then using their fantasies in creative ways. This cunningly avoids the worse peril of becoming a sexual pervert or neurotic.

The artist is likened to a child at play, living in an escapist world. 'Normal' people ought to outgrow this, and according to Freud, happy people never fantasize because it means that they are expressing unfulfilled desires. Happily, modern psychology has shown that fantasy can be positive and perfectly healthy.

Freud seems to have overlooked the fact that many artists and writers *are* neurotic and no doubt there are just as many perverts among them as there are in the general population! Taking his theory to its logical limit, if everyone's libido were fully satisfied there would be no art or literature – a depressing thought.

RELIGION

Freud wrote three books about his views on religion: *Totem and Taboo* (1912); *The Future of an Illusion* (1927); *Moses and Monotheism* (1939).

Freud noticed that many idols took on animal forms and assumed that the animal represented a protector. He observed two customs in association with these **totem** animals.

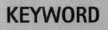

KEYWORD

Totem: an animal, plant or other object held in symbolic reverence.

❋ The animal must not be killed or eaten.

❋ An annual feast would be held, involving rituals where the animal *was* killed and eaten.

Freud suggested that laws forbidding murder and incest had their origin in such practices. A patriarchal society grows up where one particular leader has total power to decree sexual laws and taboos. This society depends upon sexual laws to define relationships between families. These laws are the basis of culture and communication. Eventually the young sons in the patriarchy rebel and kill the patriarch in order to gain power. Their resulting guilt is expressed and got rid of in the symbolic feast. This is similar to the Oedipus story. According to Freud the Moses story has the same theme. Moses was murdered by tribesmen who then experienced God's wrath. They could only escape from this uncomfortable situation by subsequent total obedience to God.

Freud claimed to be offering scientific explanations and was dismissive of religious teachings because they were not scientific. He was not interested in philosophy either, saying dismissively that it was mere playing with words. He argued that people should always try to be down to earth in their thinking and view the world objectively.

Freud always claimed to be a scientific thinker.

According to Freud the principle tasks of civilization are:

* to defend people against perils of nature, such as famine, flood and disease;

* to control and regulate instincts, such as incest, cannibalism and lust for killing;

* to demonstrate achievements that are considered worth striving for.

He suggested that Man created 'the gods' to fulfil the need for parental figures, protecting people and watching over them. Their task was:

* to protect people from the perils of nature;

* to reconcile people to the cruelty of fate, especially death;

* to compensate for the suffering imposed by civilization.

Freud was chiefly concerned with the psychological significance of the suggested functions of religion. At the heart of his criticism of religion is the fact that its teachings cannot be verified. To Freud, religious ideas are illusions, fulfilments of the oldest, most primal needs. Religious questions lead people to be introspective and not scientific, and this can lead towards self-deception. Freud does, however, rather grudgingly admit that religious teachings have undoubtedly helped to build and maintain civilization, but argued that they have also discouraged free-thinking. He also admits that he too may have been chasing an illusion, concluding that although science itself is not an illusion we may place too much emphasis upon its teachings.

PSYCHOANALYSIS TODAY

Many people have criticized Freud, saying among other things that:

* he places too much emphasis upon sex;
* he claims to be scientific and yet his findings are often vague, inaccurate and based upon small samples of data;
* many of his ideas were not actually original;
* psychoanalysis does not work – in fact it may even make symptoms worse;
* the movement has tended to have a 'closed shop' attitude – you cannot grasp the theories properly unless you are an analyst yourself;
* the theories are self-fulfilling – any attack on them can be argued to be proof that they are true – because this aggression is the result of repression.

Whatever criticism it may receive, it seems that psychoanalysis in one form or another is here to stay. It is more popular than ever, especially in America. There are many books on the subject and the ideas are now much more accessible to the general public. Its very language has become subtly absorbed into ordinary speech – we all use phrases such as 'Freudian slip', 'death wish' and 'anally retentive'. Many modern therapies have their roots in psychoanalytic thinking. Without Freud, perhaps we would not yet have begun to understand such things as:

* the importance of childhood experiences in the development of the adult personality;

* the existence of the unconscious and its huge influence over human behaviour;

* the way we all use endless defence mechanisms to protect our egos;

* the importance of dreams in understanding our true thoughts and feelings;

* the fact that talking about a problem often leads to helping to sort it out.

---

* * * *SUMMARY * * * *

● Freud said that although civilization is necessary for our growth and safety, it is difficult for people to live happily together.

● He said that war gives us a glimpse of our deep animal nature and demonstrates the working of the death instinct.

● Freud said that, artists and writers are escapists who avoid the real world by living out their fantasies.

● He said that religion is an illusion, created in order to make it easier for people to cope with life and with being members of an ordered society.

GLOSSARY

Abreaction Release of repressed emotions.

Abstract Existing in thought rather than in solid matter.

Affect Emotion attached to an idea.

Amnesia An inability to remember, either total or partial.

Aphasia A neurological disorder where the patient is either unable to recognize words, or unable to pronounce them.

Autoerotic The use of one's own body as a sexual object.

Bourgeois Middle-class, materialistic and conservative.

Cathartic method Method of therapy involving the freeing of repressed emotions.

Complex A related group of ideas that are usually repressed and cause emotional problems and conflicts.

Concrete Existing in a material form.

Condensation Fusion of two or more ideas in a dream.

Conscious mind The part of the mind that is aware of its actions and emotions.

Defence mechanisms Unconscious ways of protecting the ego against undesirable affects.

Denial Refusing to accept the reality of a situation

Determinist Someone who believes that all events follow a rigid pattern of cause and effect.

Displacement Shifting of emotions attached to an idea onto a different idea.

Dynamic model A simplified description of a system, emphasizing motives and drives.

Dynamic psychology Method that emphasizes that there are motives and drives for behaviour.

Ego The part of the psyche which reacts to external reality and which a person thinks of as the 'self'.

Eros Behaviour concerned with self-preservation and enjoyment.

Erotogenic zone An area of the body where certain stimuli, especially rubbing, produce feelings of pleasure.

Fixation Getting stuck at a particular stage in sexual development.

Free association Process where the client is given a word and then tells the analyst all the ideas that come to mind.

Free association technique Method used in psychoanalysis where the patient is encouraged to say whatever he or she feels, without censorship.

Histology Branch of anatomy dealing with the structure of tissues.

Homologous Fundamentally similar in structure and development.

Hypnosis A state similar to sleep where the patient is still able to respond to the therapist and is open to suggestions.

Hysteria A nervous disorder with varying symptoms.

Id The unconscious part of the psyche that is concerned with inherited, instinctive impulses.

Introjection Absorbing into oneself the characteristics of another person.

Latency period Period of development when sexual activity is dormant.

Latent The part of a dream that is not consciously remembered before analysis.

Libido Sexual drive.

Manifest The part of a dream that is consciously remembered.

Mechanistic view Seeing a person as a machine whose behaviour is determined by physical or chemical causes.

Neurology Branch of biology that studies the structure and functions of the nervous system.

Neuropathology The study of diseases of the nervous system.

Neurosis Minor nervous or mental disorder.

Oedipus complex Desire of the child to possess sexually the parent of the opposite sex, while excluding the parent of the same sex.

Organic disease Disease that relates to particular body structures or functions.

Overdetermined When more than one root cause is present.

Parapraxis General term for a 'Freudian slip', i.e. a slip of the tongue, or forgetting someone's name.

Philosophy A system of learning that investigates the underlying nature and truth of knowledge and existence.

Positivism A way of thinking that limits knowledge to that which is directly observable.

Preconscious The region of the mind between conscious and unconscious, where material is stored away but readily accessible.

Projection Attributing taboo urges or faults to someone else.

Psyche The mind, soul or spirit.

Psychiatry The study and treatment of mental illnesses.

Psychoanalysis The system of psychology and method of treating mental disorders.

Psychology The scientific study of the mind and behaviour.

Psychopathology A study of abnormal mental processes.

Psychosexual Relating to the mental aspects of sex, such as sexual fantasy.

Psychosis Severe mental disorder.

Rationalization Finding an excuse for behaviour that is more acceptable to the ego than the real reason.

Reaction formation Covering up an impulse by displaying the opposite behaviour.

Regression Reverting back to an earlier behaviour or developmental stage.

Repetition compulsion Inner drive that causes an individual to repeat actions.

Repressed experiences Experiences that have been actively pushed out of the conscious mind into the unconscious.

Repression Process of banishing unpleasant or undesirable feelings into the unconscious.

Resistance Process that prevents unconscious ideas from being released.

Sexual aim The sexual act that a person is driven towards.

Sexual object Person or thing from which the sexual attraction comes.

Sublimation Unconscious process by which libido is transferred to a non-sexual, socially acceptable or safe activity.

Super-ego The part of the mind that acts like an 'inner parent', giving us a conscience and responding to social rules.

Surrealism Twentieth-century art movement emphasizing unconscious and dream elements.

Symbolization Representing an object or idea by a different object or idea.

Thanatos Destructive behaviour to either the self or to others.

Totem An animal, plant or other object held in symbolic reverence.

Transference Emotional attitudes developed by the patient towards the analyst.

Unconscious Parts of the mind and personality of which a person is not aware.

Vitalist Philosophical idea that assumes non-material forces at work in biology.

FURTHER READING

There are huge numbers of books available both by and about Freud. The following brief list offers a few suggestions about where to begin further reading.

Books written by Freud:

* *The Interpretation of Dreams*, Sigmund Freud, Random House Publishing Inc, 1994

* *The Psychopathology of Everyday Life*, Penguin, 1991

* *Introductory lectures on Psychoanalysis*, Sigmund Freud, Penguin, 1973

* *New Introductory lectures on Psychoanalysis*, Sigmund Freud, Penguin, 1973

* *Moses and Monotheism*, Sigmund Freud, Random House, 1987

* *Jokes and their Relation to the Unconscious*, Sigmund Freud, WW Norton & Co, 1963

* *Three Essays on the Theory of Sexuality*, Sigmund Freud, Basic Books, 1988

* *Totem and Taboo*, Sigmund Freud, WW Norton & Co, 1989

* *Future of an Illusion*, Sigmund Freud, WW Norton & Co, 1989

* *The Standard Edition of the Complete Works of Sigmund Freud* (**24 Vol.**), Hogarth Press and the Institute of Psychoanalysis, London, 1953–74

Books about Freud:

* *The Life and Work of Sigmund Freud*, Ernest Jones, Penguin

* *Freud: A Life for Our Times*, Peter Gay, WW Norton & Co, 1998

* *Dr Freud: A Life*, Paul Ferris, Counterpoint, 1999

* *Freud*, Anthony Storr, Oxford, 1989

* *Sigmund Freud*, Stephen Wilson, Sutton, 1997

INDEX

EINSTEIN –
A BEGINNER'S GUIDE

Jim Breithaupt

Einstein – A Beginner's Guide introduces you to the great scientist and his work. No need to wrestle with difficult concepts as key ideas are presented in a clear and jargon-free way.

Jim Breithaupt's lively text:

- presents Einstein's work in historical context
- sets out the experimental evidence in support of Einstein's theories
- takes you through the theory of relativity, in simple terms
- describes the predictions from Einstein's theories on the future of the universe.

The facts … the concepts … the ideas …

JUNG – A BEGINNER'S GUIDE

Ruth Berry

Jung – A Beginner's Guide introduces you to the 'father of analytical psychology' and his work. No need to wrestle with difficult concepts as key ideas are presented in a clear and jargon-free way.

Ruth Berry's lively text explores:

- ■ Jung's background and the times he lived in
- ■ the development of Jungian analysis in simple terms
- ■ dreams and their interpretation
- ■ classic interpretations of popular myths and legends.

The facts … the concepts … the ideas …